Academic Status:

Statements and Resources

Second Edition

Edited by
Susan Kroll

Academic Status Committee
Association of College and Research Libraries
A Division of the American Library Association

Published by the Association of College and Research Libraries
A Division of the American Library Association
50 East Huron Street
Chicago, IL 60611-2795
800-545-2433

ISBN: 0-8389-7739-1

This publication is printed on recycled, acid-free paper.

Printed in the United States of America.

Table of Contents

Introduction

In 1988, the Academic Status Committee (ASC) of the Association of College and Research Libraries published *Academic Status: Statements and Resources*. The "blue book," as it came to be known, conveniently packaged all ASC model statements, guidelines, and standards that had appeared over time in *College & Research Libraries News*. This small volume rapidly became a popular favorite and demand occasioned several reprintings. Since the appearance of the blue book, the committee's work has proceeded apace and a new edition appears justified.

The policy statements that appear in this volume have been approved by the ACRL Board of Directors. Prior to Board approval, they were subjected to membership scrutiny through announcement in the literature, draft publication, open hearings, and even think tanks. The ASC has sought conscientiously to elaborate policies that meet the need and reflect the volition of the membership.

Like its predecessor, this new edition of the blue book incorporates all ASC policy statements, including the capstone 1992 revision of "Standards for Faculty Status for College and University Librarians." This was the first revision of this seminal document in the twenty-one years that had elapsed since its approval by a voice vote of the membership at Dallas in 1971.

At the 1993 Midwinter Meeting, the ALA Council, by consent, approved the incorporation of the revised "Standards" into the *ALA Handbook of Organization*. Council's exceptional action reaffirms faculty status as the desired and appropriate condition of academic librarians nationally and lends the document the support of the prestigious parent body.

From inception to realization, all members of the Academic Status Committee have contributed to this new edition. It was Susan Kroll, however, who graciously assumed responsibility for its editing and upon whose shoulders the lion's share of the production work devolved. We are in her debt.

Larry R. Oberg, Chair
ACRL Academic Status Committee
1989-1993

Standards for Faculty Status for College and University Librarians

The most pervasive characteristic of academic libraries is change. Publication continues to increase at an exponential rate and the variety of formats in which information appears is proliferating. The bibliographical apparatus of many disciplines and subdisciplines has become increasingly difficult to use as library and information technology has grown more sophisticated. For librarians to function effectively in such an environment requires flexibility, ingenuity, commitment, and a special combination of education, expertise, and experience.

The academic librarian makes unique contributions to the university community and to higher education itself. These contributions range from developing collections to providing bibliographic access to all library materials and interpreting these materials to all members of the college and university community. Specific services include instruction in the use of print and online library resources and the creation of new tools to enhance access to information available locally, regionally, nationally, or internationally. Librarians add to the sum of knowledge through their research into the information process and other areas of study. Service improvements and other advances in the field result from their participation in library and other scholarly organizations.

The intellectual contribution of the librarian who has completed formal graduate training enhances the quality of teaching, research, and public service in our colleges and universities. College and university librarians are partners with other faculty in the academic experience. A true partnership based on equivalent contributions translates to equal rights and privileges for all faculty members.

In order to recognize formally the importance of faculty status for academic librarians, the Association of College and Research Libraries, American Library Association, endorses these standards. Institutions of higher education and their governing bodies are urged to adopt these standards.

1. Professional responsibilities.
Librarians must be able to exercise independent judgment in the performance of professional duties. While librarians must have considerable latitude in fulfilling their assigned responsibilities, there must also be a regular and rigorous review of their performance. A necessary element of this review must be appraisal by a committee of peers who have access to the evidence pertaining to job performance, service, and scholarship, subject to appropriate institution policy.

2. Library governance. College and university librarians should adopt an academic form of governance similar in manner and structure to other faculties on the campus.

3. College and university governance. Librarians should be eligible for membership in the faculty senate or equivalent governing body on the

1

same basis as other faculty. They should have the same degree of representation as other academic units on all college or university governing bodies.

4. Compensation. Salaries should be comparable to and within the range of salaries paid to other faculty of equivalent rank. The appointment period for librarians should be the same as it is for equivalent faculty. Salary scales should be adjusted in an equitable manner for any additional periods of appointment. Fringe benefits should be equivalent to those for faculty in general.

5. Tenure. Librarians should be covered by tenure policies equivalent to those of other faculties. During the probationary period, librarians should have annual written contracts or agreements the same as those of other faculty.

6. Promotion. Librarians should be promoted in rank on the basis of their academic proficiency and professional effectiveness (job performance, service, and scholarship). A peer review system is the primary basis of judgment in the promotion process for academic librarians. The standards used by the library should be consistent with the campus standards for faculty.

7. Leaves. Sabbatical and other research leaves should be available to librarians on the same basis, and with the same requirements, as they are available to other faculty.

8. Research and development funds. Librarians should have access to funding for research projects and profes-

sional development on the same basis as other faculty.

9. Academic freedom. Librarians must have the same protection of academic freedom as all other faculty. Censorship of any type is unacceptable whether individual or organizational. All librarians must be free to provide access to information regardless of content.

Implementation

To implement these standards, the Association of College and Research Libraries, American Library Association, will:

1. Publicize these standards to college and university presidents and governing bodies, academic libraries, library education programs, library organizations and agencies which accredit institutions.

2. Seek to have these standards formally adopted or endorsed by the appropriate groups listed above.

3. Refer reported allegations of violations of these standards to SCRIM (Standing Committee on Review, Inquiry, and Mediation) for deliberation and consideration.

These standards become effective on the date of approval by the ACRL Board of Directors. Any library that seeks to withdraw the privileges outlined in these standards may be subject to review by the American Library Association.

Revised version passed by ACRL Board of Directors on July 3, 1991, and approved by the ALA Standards Committee in January 1992.

Model Statement for the Screening and Appointment of Academic Librarians Using a Search Committee

In colleges, universities, and other institutions of higher education, the selection and appointment of librarians rank among the most important and consequential decisions to be made. To improve the decision-making process many library administrators use a consultative arrangement in the selection process. In some cases, the administrator chiefly responsible for the final decision simply requests comments and evaluations from the appropriate individuals. In others, this process is formalized by the establishment of a search committee.[1] Consultation through a search committee solicits a breadth and range of opinion, and it facilitates objective consideration of the candidates qualifications. It also promotes a sense of participation in the selection process by interested constituencies. Because selection is a two-way process, the benefits of using a search committee accrue to the candidates as well as to the institution. Candidates receive a clear and balanced view of the institution if they have the opportunity to be interviewed by several representatives of the institution. Search committees provide a forum for discussion, including an opportunity for the development of consensus among the interviewers and for the consideration of varied representative viewpoints.

The term search committee as used in this document designates a committee constituted for the purpose of performing any or all of the functions of compiling lists of candidates for vacant positions, screening (and eliminating) candidates in accord with agreed-upon selection criteria, and recommending the list of candidates to fill the position.

The following model is provided for those institutions that choose to use search committees. Institutions recruiting without search committees may also find these procedures useful.

I. The role of the personnel officer

If the institution is large enough to have a library personnel officer, that position would be responsible for administering the search for the search committee. Normally, the personnel officer sits on all search committees (either as a member or ex-officio).

II. Formation of search committees

Search committees may be elected or appointed. In either case, the immediate goal in the formation of such committees should be to create a body representative of the constituencies affected by the position. Persons accepting appointment to the committee automatically disqualify themselves as candidates for the position.

The administrator to whom the committee is responsible should instruct the committee in writing at the outset of the process as to the following:

A. The approximate date for submission of a list of nominees and proposed date of appointment;

B. The number of finalists to be recommended;

C. The affirmative action/equal opportunity requirements;

D. The arrangements for financial and staff resources;

E. The responsibility for documenting committee actions and for preserving those records;

F. The need for confidentiality and discretion;

G. The unique concerns with respect to the position.

A copy of the position description should accompany this information.

III. Development and use of the position description or position announcement

A written position description and a summary for advertising purposes should be prepared by the supervisor of the position at the outset of the search and should serve as the standard against which candidates qualifications are judged. It should include a full account of the responsibilities and describe the educational background, experience, and competencies required or desired of the candidate. Qualifications should be written with equal opportunity and affirmative action considerations in mind.

IV. Posting the position

The responsible administrator or the chairperson should file notification of the position with the local institution and in appropriate publications, taking care that all groups protected by equal opportunity/affirmative action legislation are made aware of the vacancy. Notifications should nclude a brief description of responsibilities, qualifications, salary, description of benefits, date position is available, application deadline, name of the person to whom applications should be submitted, and a list of items to be submitted by the candidate.

V. References

A candidates references are those individuals who the candidate lists to speak or write in support of his or her candidacy. References should be requested only for those candidates under active consideration. References should be solicited from individuals whose names are provided by the applicant, and the contents should be held in strict confidence by the committee. The names of references submitted by candidates should be limited to those individuals who can provide substantive information about the candidates professional qualifications and should include, whenever possible, an administrator in the direct reporting line. Candidates are entitled to receive upon request a full list of those individuals from whom references have been solicited. Additional references may be solicited with the prior permission of the candidate. At the time of the request, referees should be advised whether or not the contents of the references will be made available to the candidate in accordance with local practice.

VI. Fair and uniform treatment

All candidates, whether external or internal to the institution, should be accorded equal treatment in the screening and interview process. The search committee should be aware of institutional guidelines when developing questions to ask the candidate before the screening and interview process.

VII. Selection and interview procedures

A. *Selection Process.*

Each committee should establish its own plan for screening and evaluating nominees and applicants consistent with library and institutionwide policies.

All applicants should be screened with reference to the qualifications and requirements stated in the position description. The purpose of initial screening is to identify and eliminate, early in the search process, nominees and applicants who are clearly unqualified. A letter should be sent to unqualified candidates stating that they will not be considered. The list of persons who remain under consideration after the initia screening should be those to whom the committee will be giving further consideration and from whom it will be seeking additional information. Fair, objective, consistent, and equitable processes should be used to narrow the field of candidates to the desired number of finalists, who will be invited for interviews.

B. *Interview Process*

Based on the candidates and the institutions needs for information, the committee and the appropriate administrative officer shall determine the composition of the interview schedule. Before the interview, the candidates should be sent information about the library and its parent organization. Such information could include guides to the library, promotion and tenure guidelines, organization charts, and bylaws.

The interview schedule should be sent to the candidate several days before the interview occurs. Both the candidate and the interviewers should recognize the constraints of time during the interview process and should follow the schedule as closely as possible.

The cost of travel, meals, and lodging for candidates invited to the campus for interviews should be borne by the inviting institution. When this is not the practice, candidates should be so apprised when an invitation is issued. If an off-campus site is selected for the interview, the candidates expenses should be paid by the inviting institution.

VIII. Recommendation of candidates

The committee should consider and evaluate in a timely manner the information gathered regarding the candidates in order to select a final list of candidates. The final list of candidates should be communicated by the chairperson to the administrator to whom the committee is responsible.

IX. Communications with candidates

Once a decision has been reached to offer the position to a particular candidate, the chief administrative officer or his/her designee should convey this information to the successful candidate. While the initial form of this communication may be oral, the official offer should be in writing and should include the specifics of the offer. The successful candidate should be allowed a reasonable period of time, acceptable to both parties, to reach a decision on the matter.[2]

A letter should be sent to unsuccessful applicants thanking them for their interest in the position and indicating that the candidate selected possessed attributes which are more congruent with the needs of the department.

X. Extending searches

If the committee is unable to reach a decision based on the applications received or if the position is readvertised with a new set of desired qualifications, all active candidates should be notified of the intention to extend the search.

XI. Announcement of appointment

Upon receipt of the successful candidates formal written acceptance, the chief administrative officer, the committee, or its designee should coordinate the announcement of the appointment with the successful candidate and should notify all other active candidates in writing.

XII. Reports, files, and records of proceedings

The responsible administrator should instruct the chairperson of the committee as to what official reports are to be filed. The chairperson should complete the necessary reports promptly and accurately. The responsible administrator should discharge the committee and thank the members for their service. The files relating to the search should be stored or disposed of in accordance with laws, regulations, and practices currently applicable in the local setting.

---

1. See "Model Statement of Criteria and Procedures for Appointment, Promotion in Academic Rank, and Tenure for College and University Librarians," *College and Research Libraries News* (May 1987).
2. Ibid.

Approved by the membership of the Association of College and Research Libraries, a division of the American Library Association, June 26, 1972.

Copies of the statement are available upon request from the ACRL office, 50 E. Huron St., Chicago, IL 60611-2795.

Joint Statement on Faculty Status of College and University Librarians

As the primary means through which students and faculty gain access to the storehouse of organized knowledge, the college and university library performs a unique and indispensable function in the educational process. This function will grow in importance as students assume greater responsibility for their own intellectual and social development. Indeed all members of the academic community are likely to become increasingly dependent on skilled professional guidance in the acquisition and use of library resources as the forms and numbers of these resources multiply, scholarly materials appear in more languages, bibliographical systems become more complicated, and library technology grows increasingly sophisticated. The librarian who provides such guidance plays a major role in the learning process.

The character and quality of the institution of higher learning are shaped in large measure by the nature of its library holdings and the ease and imagination with which those resources are made accessible to members of the academic community. Consequently, all members of the faculty should take an active interest in the operation and development of the library. Because the scope and character of library resources should be taken into account in such important academic decisions as curricular planning and faculty appointments, librarians should have a voice in the development of the institution's educational policy.

Librarians perform a teaching and research role in as much as they instruct students formally and informally and advise and assist faculty in their scholarly pursuits. Librarians are also themselves involved in the research function; many conduct research in their own professional interests and in the discharge of their duties.

Where the role of college and university librarians, as described in the preceding paragraph, requires them to function essentially as part of the faculty, this functional identity should be recognized by granting of faculty status. Neither administrative responsibilities nor professional degrees, titles, or skills, per se, qualify members of the academic community for faculty status. The *function* of the librarian as participant in the processes of teaching and research is the essential criterion of faculty status.

College and university librarians share the professional concerns of faculty members. Academic freedom, for example, is indispensable to librarians, because they are trustees of knowledge with the responsibility of insuring the availability of information and ideas, no matter how controversial, so that teachers may freely teach and students may freely learn. Moreover, as members of the academic community, librarians should have latitude in the exercise of their professional judgement within the library, a share in shaping policy within the institution, and adequate opportunities for professional development and appropriate reward.

Faculty status entails for librarians the same rights and responsibilities as for other members of the faculty. They should have corresponding entitlement to rank, promotion, tenure, compensation, leaves, and research funds. They must go through the same process of evaluation and meet the same standards as other faculty members.[1]

On some campuses, adequate procedures for extending faculty status to librarians have already been worked out. These procedures vary from campus to campus because of institutional differences. In the development of such procedures, it is essential that the general faculty or its delegated agent determine the specific steps by which any professional position is to be accorded faculty rank and status. In any case, academic positions which are to be accorded faculty rank and status should be approved by the senate or the faculty at large before submission to the president and to the governing board for approval.

With respect to library governance, it is to be presumed that the governing board, the administrative officers, the library faculty, and representatives of the general faculty, will share in the determination of library policies that affect the general interests of the institution and its educational program. In matters of internal governance, the library will operate like other academic units with respect to decisions relating to appointments, promotions, tenure, and conditions of service.[2]

---

1. Cf. "1940 Statement of Principles on Academic Freedom and Tenure"; "1958 Statement on Procedural Standards in Faculty Dismissal Proceedings"; "1972 Statement on Leaves of Absence".

2. Cf. "1966 Statement on Government of Colleges and Universities", formulated by the American Council on Education, American Association of University Professors, and Association of Governing Boards of Universities and Colleges.

Drafted by a committee of the Association of College and Research Libraries (ACRL), the Association of American Colleges (AAC), and the American Association of University Professors (AAUP).

Guidelines for Academic Status for College and University Libraries

In 1971 the Association of College and Research Libraries (ACRL) adopted the ACRL Standards for Faculty Status of College and University Librarians. ACRL supports faculty rank, status, and tenure for librarians and has developed the following guidelines in support of this concept:

1. ACRL Guidelines and Procedures for Screening and Appointment of Academic Librarians (1977).

2. ACRL/AAUP/AAC Joint Statement on Faculty Status of College and University Librarians (1972).

3. ACRL Model Statement of Criteria and Procedures for Appointment, Promotion in Academic Rank, and Tenure for College and University Librarians (1987).

For those institutions which have not yet achieved faculty rank, status, and tenure for academic librarians, ACRL has developed the guidelines for academic status listed below to ensure that the rights, privileges and responsibilities of librarians in all institutional settings continue to reflect that these professionals are an integral part of the academic mission of the institutions in which they serve.

1. Professional responsibilities. Librarians should be assigned general responsibilities within their particular area of competence. They should have maximum latitude in fulfilling these responsibilities. Their performance of these responsibilities should be regularly and vigorously reviewed by committees of their peers as well as by supervisory personnel. Review standards should be published and uniformly applied; reviewing bodies should have access to all appropriate documentation.

2. Governance. Librarians should participate in the development of policies and procedures for the Library, and in the hiring, review, retention, and continuing appointment processes for their peers. Because the library exists to support the teaching and research functions of the institution, librarians should participate in the development of the institution's educational policy, have a role in curricular planning, and be a part of the institution's governance structure.

3. Contracts. A librarian's appointment should be by written contract, agreement, or letter of appointment of no less than one year in duration. The appointment document should state the terms and conditions of service and grant security of employment for the contractual period. After a probationary period of no longer than seven years and through a process which includes peer review, librarians should be granted continuing employment if they have met the appropriate conditions and standards.

4. Compensation. The salary scale and benefits for librarians should be the same as for other academic categories with equivalent education, experience, or responsibility.

5. Promotion and salary increases. Librarians should be promoted through ranks on the basis of their professional proficiency and effectiveness. A peer review system should be an integral part of procedures for promotion and decisions on salary increases. The librarians' promotion ladder should have equivalent titles and ranks as that of the faculty.

6. Leaves and research funds. Librarians should be eligible for research funds within the University, and encouraged to apply for such funds from sources outside the University. University and library administrations should provide leaves of absence, sabbaticals, and other means of administrative support to promote the active participation of librarians in research and other professional activities.

7. Academic freedom. Librarians are entitled to the protection of academic freedom as set forth in the 1940 Statement of Principles on Academic Freedom and Tenure of the American Association of University Professors.

8. Dismissal or nonreappointment. Dismissal of librarians during the terms of appointment may be effected by the institution only for just cause and through academic due process. Nonreappointment should involve adequate notice, peer review, and access to a grievance procedure.

9. Grievance. Grievance procedures should be accessible to librarians and should include steps to be completed within specified time limits, effective safeguards against reprisal by the institution, or abuse of the procedures by the grievant, and must be consistent with applicable institutional regulations and contracts.

The final version approved by the ACRL Board at the 1990 Midwinter Meeting.

Model Statement of Criteria and Procedures for Appointment, Promotion in Academic Rank, and Tenure for College and University Librarians

Introduction

This Model Statement of Criteria and Procedures is intended for use within the context of two ACRL policy statements on faculty status for academic librarians[1], as well as related statements issued by the American Association of University Professors.[2] The objective of this Model Statement is to propose criteria and procedures for appointment, promotion in academic rank, and tenure for use in academic libraries which will insure that the Library Faculty and, therefore, library services, at an institution utilizing these criteria and procedures will be of the highest quality possible, consistent with the goals and resources of the institution. These criteria are intended to be minimal only. These procedures may need to be adjusted in minor detail to conform with existing institutional procedures for other faculty. If there are contractual procedures in existence, they must be observed.

I. Appointment

A. *General Policies*

1. Appointment of librarians shall follow the same procedures that are established for appointing all faculty. Any librarian appointed to a college or university Library Faculty shall have the appropriate terminal professional degree.[3] Appointment to any rank shall meet the criteria appropriate to that rank.

2. To insure that only candidates of the highest quality are appointed to the Library Faculties of colleges and universities, there shall be a committee or committees, representative of the Library Faculty and appropriately selected, which shall review all candidates for appointment to the Library Faculty. This committee (or these committees) shall screen the candidates, participate in the interview process, and make recommendations to the appropriate administrative officer of the library concerning appointment and initial assignment of rank.

3. The terms and conditions of every appointment to the Library Faculty shall be stated and confirmed in writing, and copies of all relevant documents, including the official document of appointment, shall be given to the faculty member. Subsequent extensions or modifications of an appointment, and any special understandings or notices incumbent on either party to provide, shall be stated and confirmed in writing and copies shall be given to the faculty member.

4. Copies of the appointment document, countersigned by the appropriate institutional officer and the faculty member, shall be held by both the institution and the individual when an appointment becomes effective.

B. *Probationary Appointments*

1. Probationary appointments may be for one year, or for other stated periods, subject to renewal. The total

period of full-time service prior to the acquisition of continuous tenure shall not exceed _ years,[4] and may include previous full-time service with the rank of instructor or higher in other institutions of higher learning (except that the probationary period may extend to as much as four years, even if the total full-time service in the profession thereby exceeds seven years; the terms of such extension shall be stated in writing at the time of initial appointment).[5] Scholarly leave of absence for one year or less shall count as part of the probationary period as if it were prior service at another institution, unless the individual and the institution agree in writing to an exception to this provision at the time the leave is granted.

2. The faculty member shall be advised, at the time of initial appointment, of the substantive standards and procedures generally employed in decisions affecting renewal and tenure. Any special standards adopted by the library shall also be transmitted. The faculty member shall be advised of the time when decisions affecting renewal or tenure are ordinarily made, and shall be given the opportunity to submit material believed to be helpful to an adequate consideration of the faculty member's circumstances.

3. Regardless of the stated term or other provisions of any appointments, written notice that probationary appointment is not to be renewed shall be given to the faculty member in advance of the expiration of the appointment, as follows: (a) Not later than March 1 of the first academic year of service if the appointment expires at the end of that academic year; or, if a one-year appointment termi-

nates during an academic year, at least three months in advance of its termination; (b) not later than December 15 of the second academic year of service if the appointment expires at the end of that year; or, if an initial two-year appointment terminates during an academic year, at least six months in advance of its termination; (c) at least twelve months before the expiration of an appointment after two or more years of service at the institution. The institution shall normally notify faculty members of the terms and conditions of their renewals by March 15, but in no case shall such information be given later than _____.[6]

4. When a faculty recommendation or a decision not to renew an appointment has first been reached, the faculty member involved shall be informed of that recommendation or decision in writing by the body or individual making the initial recommendation or decision; the faculty member shall be advised upon request of the reasons which contributed to that decision. The faculty member may request a reconsideration by the recommending or deciding body.

5. If the faculty member so requests, the reasons given in explanation of the nonrenewal shall be confirmed in writing.

6. Insofar as the faculty member alleges that the decision against renewal by the appropriate faculty body was based on inadequate consideration, the committee which reviews the faculty member's allegation shall determine whether the decision was the result of adequate consideration in terms of the relevant standards of the institution. The review committee shall not substitute its judgment on the merits for that of the faculty body. If the

review committee believes that adequate consideration was not given to the faculty member's qualifications, it shall request reconsideration by the faculty body, indicating the respects in which it believes the consideration may have been inadequate. It shall provide copies of its findings to the faculty member, the faculty body, and the president or other appropriate administrative officer.

II. Promotion in academic rank

A. *General Professional and Scholarly Qualifications of the Library Faculty*

The librarian's academic preparation for an appointment to the Library Faculty is established on the basis of the terminal professional degree. The basic quality which must be evident for promotion in academic rank is the ability to perform at a high professional level in areas which contribute to the educational and research mission of the institution, such as: reference service, collection development, bibliographic organization and control.

Evidence of this level of performance may be adduced from the judgments of colleagues on the Library Faculty, from members of the academic community outside the library, and/or from professional colleagues outside the academic institution.

Additional evidence for promotion in rank may include:

1. Contributions to the educational function of the university: for example, teaching, not necessarily in a classroom situation; organization of workshops, institutes or similar meetings; public appearances in the interest of librarianship or information transfer. Evaluation of such activities may be on the basis of the judgment of those who are instructed and by the considered opinion of colleagues.

2. Contributions to the advancement of the profession: for example, active participation in professional and learned societies as a member, as an officer, as a committee member, or as committee member, or as a committee chairperson.

3. Activities related to inquiry and research: for example, publications, such as in professional and scholarly journals; presentation of papers; reviews of books and other literature; grants; consulting; service as a member of a team of experts task force, review committee or similar body. Such activities shall be judged by professional colleagues on and/or off the campus on the basis of their contribution to scholarship, the profession of librarianship, and library service.

B. *Criteria for Promotion to Specific Ranks*

Promotion to the ranks of assistant professor, associate professor, and professor requires a record of successful fulfillment of criteria at the lower level.

Instructor—Appointments at this rank shall require expectation of successful overall performance and the potential for a promising career in librarianship.

Assistant professor—Promotion to this rank shall require evidence of significant professional contributions to the library and/or to the institution.

Associate professor—Promotion to this rank shall require evidence of substantial professional contributions to the library and to the institution as well as attainment of a high level in bibliographical activities, in research, or in other professional endeavors.

Professor—Promotion to this rank shall require outstanding achievements in bibliographical activities, in research, or in other professional endeavors.

C. *Procedures for Promotion to Specific Ranks*

1. All those below the rank of professor shall be reviewed for promotion according to the procedures of the institution.

2. Candidates from the Library Faculty for promotion in academic rank shall be considered by a standing or ad hoc peer review committee formed in accordance with appropriate institutional regulations. In the absence of specific regulations, such a committee could be selected by the Library Faculty or appointed by the chief administrative officer on the basis of recommendations from the Library Faculty.

3. Recommendations for promotion in academic rank may be made by the appropriate library department head, the appropriate assistant or associate director, or a member of the Library Faculty. The candidate shall receive copies of any recommendations or evaluations by the department head, appropriate assistant or associate director, and the chief administrative officer of the library. These statements shall become part of the permanent record.

4. Documentation in support of candidates for promotion in rank shall include evaluations from the appropriate library department head, assistant or associate director. Additional documentation may include letters from colleagues, copies of publications and/or reviews, records of committee activity and the like.

5. The ad hoc or standing committee (see C-2) shall transmit its recommendations to the chief administrative officer of the library for all candidates together with all supporting documentation.

6. The chief administrative officer of the library will receive the recommendations of the committee, will make his/her decision, and so notify the committee. If the chief administrative officer of the library does not concur in any particular recommendation, he/she may, after consultation with the committee, note such disagreement before notifying the candidate of the recommendations. The chief administrative officer of the library shall inform the committee and the candidate in writing of the recommendations before transmitting the recommendations of the committee and the chief administrative officer of the library to the appropriate institutional officer. The candidate will then have the opportunity to respond in writing to the recommendations. After this, the chief administrative officer of the library will submit his/her recommendation, the recommendation of the committee, and any responses from these parties or from the candidate, to the appropriate institutional officer.

7. If a member of the Library Faculty believes there are substantial grounds for disagreement with a denial of promotion, appropriate institutional regulations shall be provided so that the case may be properly reviewed.

III. Tenure (continuous appointment)

A. Tenure is defined as an institutional commitment to permanent and continuous employment to be terminated only for adequate cause (for example, incompetence; moral turpitude; retirement for reasons of age, mental or physical disability; bona fide financial exigency) and only after due process. Tenure (continuous appointment) shall be available to librarians in accordance with the tenure provision of all faculty of the institution.

B. The criteria for tenure are closely allied to the criteria for promotion in academic rank. The relationship between tenure and rank shall be the same for Library Faculty as for other faculty in the institution. These criteria include:

1. effectiveness of performance as a librarian;

2. quality of scholarship;

3. effectiveness of professional service.

C. A member of the Library Faculty who is a candidate for tenure shall be reviewed according to procedures set forth in established institutional regulations as applied to other faculty on the campus. These procedures shall be similar to those described above for promotion in academic rank.

IV. Termination of appointments

A. *Notification*

Faculty members may terminate their appointments, provided they give notice in writing at the earliest possible opportunity, or 30 days after receiving notification of the terms of appointment for the coming year. Faculty members may properly request a waiver of this requirement of notice in case of hardship or in a situation where they would otherwise be denied substantial professional advancement or other opportunity.

B. *Termination of Appointment by the Institution*

1. Termination of an appointment with continuous tenure, or of a probationary or special appointment before the end of the specified term, may be effected by the institution only for adequate cause.

2. If termination takes the form of a dismissal for cause, it shall be pursuant to the procedure specified in section VI below.

C. *Financial Exigency*

1. Termination of an appointment with continuous tenure, or of a probationary or special appointment before the end of the specified term, may occur under extraordinary circumstances because of a demonstrably bona fide financial exigency, i.e., an imminent financial crisis which threatens the survival of the institution as a whole and which cannot be alleviated by less drastic means.

[*NOTE*: Each institution in adopting regulations on financial exigency will need to decide how to share and allocate the hard judgments and decisions that are necessary in such a crisis.

As a first step, there shall be a faculty body which participates in the decision that a condition of financial exigency exists or is imminent, and that all feasible alternatives to termination of appointments have been pursued.

Judgments determining where within the overall academic program termination of appointments may occur involve considerations of educational policy, including affirmative action, as well as of faculty status; and shall therefore be the primary responsibility of the faculty or of an appropriate faculty body. The faculty or an appropriate faculty body shall also exercise primary responsibility in determining the criteria for identifying the individuals whose appointments are to be terminated. The criteria may appropriately include considerations of age and of length of service.

The responsibility for identifying individuals whose appointments are to be terminated shall be committed to a person or group designated or approved by the faculty. The allocation of this responsibility may vary according to the size and character of the institution, the extent of the terminations to be made, or other considerations of fairness in judgment. The case of a faculty member given notice of proposed termination of appointment will be governed by the following procedure.]

2. If the administration issues notice to a particular faculty member of an intention to terminate the appointment because of financial exigency, the faculty member shall have the right to a full hearing before a faculty committee. The hearing need not conform in all respects with a proceeding conducted pursuant to Section VI, but the essentials of an on-the-record adjudicative hearing shall be observed. The issues in this hearing may include:

a. The existence and extent of the condition of financial exigency. The burden will rest on the administration to prove the existence and extent of the condition. The findings of a faculty committee in a previous proceeding involving the same issue may be introduced.

b. The validity of the educational judgements and the criteria for iden-tification for termination, but the recommendations of a faculty body on these matters shall be considered presumptively valid.

c. Whether the criteria are being properly applied in the individual case.

3. If the institution, because of financial exigency, terminates appointments, it shall not at the same time make new appointments except in extraordinary circumstances where a serious distortion in the academic program would otherwise result. The appointment of a faculty member with tenure shall not be terminated in favor of retaining a faculty member without tenure, except in extraordinary circumstances where a serious distortion of the academic program would otherwise result.

4. Before terminating an appointment because of financial exigency, the institution, with faculty participation, shall make every effort to place the faculty member concerned in another suitable position within the institution.

5. In all cases of termination of appointment because of financial exigency, the faculty member concerned shall be given notice or severance salary not less than as prescribed in Section IX.

6. In all cases of termination of appointment because of financial exigency, the place of the faculty member concerned shall not be filled by a replacement within a period of three years, unless the released faculty member has been offered reinstatement and a reasonable time in which to accept or decline it.

D. *Discontinuation of a Program or Department Not Mandated by Financial Exigency*

Termination of an appointment with continuous tenure, or a probationary or special appointment before the end of the specified term, may occur as a result of bona fide formal discontinuance of a program or department of instruction. The following standards and procedures shall apply:

1. The decision to discontinue formally a program or department of instruction shall be based essentially upon educational considerations as determined primarily by the faculty as a whole or an appropriate committee thereof.

[*NOTE*: "Educational considerations" do not include cyclical or temporary variations in enrollment. They must reflect long-range judgments that the educational mission of the institution as a whole will be enhanced by the discontinuance.]

2. Before the administration issues notice to a faculty member of its intention to terminate an appointment because of formal discontinuance of a program or department of instruction, the institution shall make every effort to place the faculty member concerned in another suitable position. If placement in another position is facilitated by a reasonable period of training, financial and other support for such training will be proffered. If no position is available within the institution, with or without retraining, the faculty member's appointment then may be terminated, but only with provision for severance salary equitably adjusted to the faculty member's length of past and potential service.

[*NOTE*: When an institution proposes to discontinue a program or department of instruction, it should plan to bear the costs of relocating, training, or otherwise compensating faculty members adversely affected.]

3. A faculty member may appeal a proposed relocation or termination resulting from a discontinuance and has a right to a full hearing before a faculty committee. The hearing need not conform in all respects with a proceeding conducted pursuant to Section VI but the essentials of an on-the-record adjudicative hearing shall be observed. The issues in such a hearing may include the institution's failure to satisfy any of the conditions specified in this section. In such a hearing a faculty determination that a program or department is to be discontinued shall be considered presumptively valid, but the burden of proof on other issues shall rest on the administration.

E. *Termination for Medical Reasons*

Termination of an appointment with tenure, or of a probationary or special appointment before the end of the period of appointment, for medical reasons, shall be based upon clear and convincing medical evidence that the faculty member cannot continue to fulfill the terms and conditions of the appointment. The decision to terminate shall be reached only after there has been appropriate consultation and after the faculty member concerned, or someone representing the faculty member, has been informed of the basis of the proposed action and has been afforded an opportunity to present the faculty member's position and to respond to the evidence. If the faculty member so requests, the evidence shall be reviewed by the appropriate committee before a final decision is made by the governing board on the recommendation of the administration. The faculty member shall be given severance salary not less than as prescribed in Section IX.

F. *Review*

In case of termination of appointment, the governing board will be available for ultimate review.

V. Grievance

In the event that an amicable solution cannot be reached between the two parties, a grievance procedure shall be provided by the institution. The general criteria for a grievance procedure include:

A. The grievance procedure shall be equitable to the institution and to the individual.

B. The grievance procedure shall state clearly what is to be done, when, and by whom.

C. The term "grievance" shall be clearly defined, Any other terms which could be misunderstood shall also be defined.

D. Grievance procedures shall be easy to initiate and accessible to all members of the Library Faculty.

E. Steps in the grievance procedure shall be completed within specified time limits which do not allow either party to delay proceedings unduly. More time shall be allowed as the grievance moves to higher levels in the procedure.

F. There shall be effective safeguards against reprisal for initiating or participating in a grievance proceeding and against abuse of the procedures by the grievant or by the institution.

G. Excessive reliance on precedent is undesirable.

H. Any grievance procedure in a library must be consistent with applicable institutional regulations and contracts.

VI. Dismissal procedures

A. Adequate cause for a dismissal shall be related, directly and substantially, to the fitness of faculty members in their professional capacities as librarians. Dismissal shall not be used to restrain faculty members in their exercise of academic freedom or of other rights of American citizens.

B. Dismissal of a faculty member with continuous tenure, or with a special or probationary appointment before the end of the specified term, shall be preceded by:

1. discussions between the faculty member and appropriate administrative officers looking toward a mutual settlement;

2. informal inquiry by the duly elected faculty committee that may, failing to effect an adjustment, determine whether in its opinion dismissal proceedings shall be undertaken, without its opinion being binding upon the president;

3. a statement of charges, framed with reasonable particularity by the president or the president's delegate.

C. A dismissal, as defined above, shall be preceded by a statement of reasons, and the individual concerned shall have the right to be heard initially by the elected faculty hearing committee.[7] Members deeming themselves disqualified for bias or interest shall remove themselves from the case, either at the request of a party or on their own initiative. Each party shall have a maximum of two challenges without stated cause.[8]

1. Pending a final decision by the hearing committee, the faculty member shall be suspended, or assigned to other duties in lieu of suspension, only if immediate harm to the faculty member or others is threatened by continuance. Before suspending a faculty member, pending an ultimate determination of the faculty member's status through the institution's hearing procedures, the administration shall consult with the appropriate committee concerning the propriety, the length, and the other conditions of the suspension. A suspension which is intended to be final is a dismissal, and shall be treated as such. Salary shall continue during the period of the suspension.

2. The hearing committee may, with the consent of the parties concerned, hold joint prehearing meetings with the parties to:

a. simplify the issues;

b. effect stipulations of facts;

c. provide for the exchange of documentary or other information; and,

d. achieve such other appropriate prehearing objectives as shall make the hearing fair, effective, and expeditious.

3. Service of notice of hearing with specific charges in writing shall be made at least twenty days prior to the hearing. The faculty member may waive a hearing or may respond to the charges in writing at any time before the hearing. If the faculty member waives a hearing, but denies the charges or asserts that the charges do not support a finding of adequate cause, the hearing tribunal shall evaluate all available evidence and rest its recommendation upon the evidence in the record.

4. The committee, in consultation with the president and the faculty member, shall exercise its judgment as to whether the hearing shall be public or private.

5. During the proceedings the faculty member shall be permitted to have an academic advisor and counsel of the faculty member's choice.

6. At the request of either party or the hearing committee, a representative of a responsible educational association shall be permitted to attend the proceedings as an observer.

7. A verbatim record of the hearing or hearings shall be taken and a typewritten copy shall be made available to the faculty member without cost, at the faculty member's request.

8. The burden of proof that adequate cause exists rests with the institution and shall be satisfied only by clear and convincing evidence in the record considered as a whole.

9. The hearing committee shall grant adjournments to enable either party to investigate evidence as to which a valid claim of surprise is made.

10. The faculty member shall be afforded an opportunity to obtain necessary witnesses, documentation, or other evidence. The administration shall cooperate with the hearing committee in securing witnesses and making available documentation and other evidence.

11. The faculty member and the administration shall have the right to confront and cross-examine all witnesses. Where the witnesses cannot or shall not appear, but the committee determines that the interests of justice require admission of their statements, the committee shall identify the witnesses, disclose their statements, and, if possible, provide for interrogatories.

12. In the hearing of charges of incompetence, the testimony shall include that of qualified faculty members from this or other institutions of higher education.

13. The hearing committee shall not be bound by strict rules of legal evidence, and may admit any evidence which is of probative value in determining the issues involved. Every possible effort shall be made to obtain the most reliable evidence available.

14. The findings of fact and the decision shall be based solely on the hearing record.

15. Except for such simple announcements as may be required, covering the time of the hearing and similar matters, public statements and publicity about the case by either the faculty member or administrative officers shall be avoided so far as possible until the proceedings have been completed, including consideration by the governing board of the institution. The president and the faculty member shall be notified of the decision in writing and shall be given a copy of the record of the hearing.

16. If the hearing committee concludes that adequate cause for dismissal has not been established by the evidence in the record, it shall so report to the president. If the president rejects the report, the president shall state the reasons for doing so, in writing, to the hearing committee and to the faculty member, and provide an opportunity for response before transmitting the case to the governing board. If the hearing committee concludes that adequate cause for a dismissal has been established, but that an academic penalty less than dismissal is more appropriate, it shall so recommend, with supporting reasons.

VII. Action by the governing board

If dismissal or other severe sanction is recommended, the president shall, on request of the faculty member, transmit to the governing board the record of the case. The governing board's review shall be based on the record of the committee hearing, and it shall provide opportunity for argument, oral or written or both, by the principals at the hearings or by their representatives. The decision of the hearing committee shall either be sustained, or the proceeding returned to the committee with specific objections. The committee shall then reconsider; taking into account the stated objections, and receiving new evidence if necessary. The governing board shall make a final decision only after study of the committee's reconsideration.

VIII. Procedures for imposition of sanctions other than dismissal

A. If the administration believes that the conduct of a faculty member, although not constituting adequate cause for dismissal, is sufficiently grave to justify imposition of a severe sanction, such as suspension from service for a stated period, the administration may institute a proceeding to impose such a severe sanction; the procedures outlined in Section VI shall govern such a proceeding.

B. If the administration believes that the conduct of a faculty member justifies the imposition of a minor sanction, such as a reprimand, it shall notify the faculty member of the basis of the proposed sanction and provide the faculty member with an opportunity to persuade the administration that the proposed sanction shall not be imposed. A faculty member who believes that a major sanction has been incorrectly imposed under this paragraph, or that a minor sanction has been unjustly imposed, may, pursuant to Section V, petition the faculty grievance committee for such action as may be appropriate.

IX. Terminal salary or notice

If the appointment is terminated, the faculty member shall receive salary or notice in accordance with the following schedule: at least three months, if the final decision is reached by March 1 (or three months prior to the expiration of the first year of probationary service); at least six months if the decision is reached by December 15 of the second year (or after nine months but prior to eighteen months) of probationary service; at least one year, if the decision is reached after eighteen months of probationary service or if the faculty member has tenure. This provision for terminal notice or salary need not apply in the event that there has been a finding that the conduct which justified dismissal involved moral turpitude. On the recom-

mendation of the faculty hearing committee or the president, the governing board, in determining what, if any, payments shall be made beyond the effective date of dismissal, may take into account the length and quality of service of the faculty member.

X. Academic freedom and protection against discrimination

A. All members of the faculty, whether tenured or not, are entitled to academic freedom as set forth in the 1940 "Statement of Principles on Academic Freedom and Tenure," formulated by the Association of American Colleges and the American Association of University Professors.

B. All members of the faculty, whether tenured or not, are entitled to protection against illegal or unconstitutional discrimination by the institution, or discrimination on a basis not demonstrably related to the faculty member's professional performance, including but not limited to race, sex, religion, national origin, age, physical handicap, marital status, or sexual or affectional preference.

XI. Complaints of violation of academic freedom or of discrimination in nonreappointment

If a faculty member on probationary or other nontenured appointment alleges that a decision against reappointment was based significantly on considerations violative of (1) academic freedom or (2) governing policies on making appointments without prejudice with respect to race, sex, religion, national origin, age, physical handicap, marital status, or sexual or affectional preference, the allegation shall be given preliminary consideration by the appropriate committee, which shall seek to settle the matter by informal methods. The allegation shall be accompanied by a statement that the faculty member agrees to the presentation, for the consideration of the faculty committee, of such reasons and evidence as the institution may allege in support of its decision. If the difficulty is unresolved at this stage, and if the committee so recommends, the matter shall be heard in the manner set forth in Sections VI and VII, except that the faculty member making the complaint is responsible for stating the grounds upon which the allegations are based, and the burden of proof shall rest upon the faculty member. If the faculty member succeeds in establishing a prima facie case, it is incumbent upon those who made their decision against reappointment to come forward with evidence in support of the decision. Statistical evidence of improper discrimination may be used in establishing a prima facie case.

XII. Administrative personnel

The foregoing regulations apply to administrative personnel who hold academic rank, but only in their capacity as faculty members. Administrators who allege that a consideration violative of academic freedom, or of governing policies against improper discrimination as stated in Section XI, significantly contributed to a decision to terminate their appointment to an administrative post, or not to reappoint them, are entitled to the procedures set forth in Section XI.

XIII. Political activities of faculty members

Faculty members, as citizens, are free to engage in political activities. Where necessary, leaves of absence may be given for the duration of an election campaign or a term of office, on timely application, and for a reasonable period of time. The terms of such leaves of absence shall be set forth in writing, and the leave shall not affect unfavorably the tenure status of a faculty member, except that time spent on such leave shall not count as probationary service unless otherwise agreed to.

---

1. "Standards for Faculty Status for College and University Librarians," adopted by the Membership of the Association of College and Research Libraries, Dallas, Texas, June 26, 1971;" Joint Statement on Faculty Status of College and University Librarians," drafted by a committee of the Association of American Colleges (AAC), the American Association of University Professors (AAUP) and the Association of College and Research Libraries (ACRL) on April 26, 1972; endorsed by ACRL Membership, Chicago, Illinois, June 26, 1972, and by AAUP Membership, St. Louis, Missouri, April 1973.

2. "1982 Recommended Institutional Regulations on Academic Freedom and Tenure," *AAUP Policy Documents & Reports* (1984 ed.), pp. 21–30. Much of the present document has been drawn from this statement. In particular, the following sections have been adopted nearly in their entirety: section IV (Termination of Appointments); VI (Dismissal Procedures); VII (Action by the Governing Board); VIII

(Procedures for Imposition of Sanctions Other Than Dismissal); IX (Terminal Salary or Notice); X (Academic Freedom and Protection Against Discrimination); XI (Complaints of Violation of Academic Freedom or of Discrimination in Nonreappointment); XII (Administrative Personnel); XIII (Political Activities of Faculty Members).

3. See the "ACRL Statement on the Terminal Professional Degree for Academic Librarians."

4. This period will not normally exceed seven years.

5. The exception here noted applies only to an institution whose maximum probationary period exceeds four years.

6. April 15 is the recommended date.

7. This shall not be the same committee as constituted in section B above.

8. Regulations of the institution shall provide for alternates, or for some other method of filling vacancies on the hearing committee resulting from disqualification, challenge without stated cause, illness, resignation or other reason.

This statement is a revision of the Model Statement first issued by ACRL in 1973. Revised by the Academic Status Committee, the new statement was approved for publication by the Board of Directors of the Association of College and Research Libraries on January 20, 1987, during the Midwinter Meeting in Chicago. The previous version, published in College and Research Libraries News in September and October 1973, was rescinded.

Statement on Collective Bargaining

The policy of the Association of College and Research Libraries is that academic librarians shall be included on the same basis as their faculty colleagues in units for collective bargaining. Such units shall be guided by the standards and guidelines pertaining to faculty and academic status of the Association of College and Research Libraries.

Developed by the ACRL Academic Status Committee; approved by the ACRL Board of Directors and the ALA Standards Committee at the 1993 Midwinter Meeting.

Statement on the Terminal Professional Degree for Academic Librarians

The master's degree in library science from a library school program accredited by the American Library Association is the appropriate terminal professional degree for academic librarians.

Approved as policy by the Board of Directors of the Association of College and Research Libraries, a division of the American Library Association, on January 23, 1975.

A Bibliographic Essay On Faculty Status For Academic Librarians

Janet Krompart

Introduction

Libraries always have been insepa-rable from higher education; and, in the United States at least, the first academic librarians were drawn from the ranks of the faculty. This tradition of college and university libraries managed by faculty lasted at least to the end of the 19th century when the establishment of the College Library Section of the American Library Association in 1889 marked the recognition of academic librarianship as a profession. It is not surprising, there-fore, that even before 20th century tech-nology and high publication rates made plain the need for professionally-trained librarians, the question of academic li-brarian status, vis-à-vis faculty in par-ticular, appeared in writings on library management.[1]

Following these 19th century be-ginnings, the debate continued. And, when interest in improving librarians' status and conditions of work increased after World War II, the rate of status publication also grew. The creation of the Committee on Academic Status (now the Academic Status Committee; here-after ASC) of the Association of Col-lege and Research Libraries in 1959 and the establishment of the 1971 Stan-dards for Faculty Status for College and University Librarians (hereafter the Standards)[2] were early milestones in several decades of high interest and continuous status publication.

Because the topics that belong to faculty status literature cannot be de-fined precisely, it is not easy to count these materials. Writings on collec-tive bargaining, professionalism, re-search, etc. sometimes are included, sometimes not. The rate of faculty status publication, however, may be estimated conservatively as ten titles per year through the 1980s into the present.[3]

In spite of this history of prolific status publications, a strong, stable role for librarians in academe has not been widely realized or even gener-ally agreed upon; and "academic limbo," a term that was first applied to librarians' status in 1974[4] still fits the situation described by many cur-rent writers.[5] With prospects for solution further dimmed by difficult economic times, the problem seems intractable. The literature, however, is rich in history and insights that promise a challenging and reward-ing, if not comfortable, future.

The bibliography of faculty sta-tus has been recorded elsewhere.[6] The purpose of this chapter is to track patterns in status literature from the 1971 promulgation of the Standards to the present. The first section con-tains a discussion of the source mate-rials and the most persistent or recur-ring themes of faculty status litera-ture. A brief examination of some

Janet Krompart is Collection Development Coordinator at Oakland Univer-sity Library, Rochester, Michigan.

topics and views readers might expect to find that have *not* been addressed follows. The concluding section describes current writing about strengthening the position of libraries and librarians in academe.

Source materials and notable themes in faculty status literature

Each of the topics discussed below has sufficient coverage in the literature to constitute an important part of status writings; and all are well-represented in post-1971 publications. The Standards and the writings that record librarians' actual circumstances (Item no. 1) are primary source material, and Items 1-3 together present the most basic and persistent faculty status themes. Items 4-5, while significant and perhaps of special importance for the future, have received less coverage.

1. Source materials.

The Standards, the documents of the ASC, and the faculty status surveys and other records of librarians' working conditions are the core of status literature. Taken together these materials present both the stated goal for librarians' status and the actual circumstances of working librarians and illuminate the unresolved questions about librarians' role in academe.

The Association of College and Research Libraries' work to resolve the question of librarian status and to strengthen librarians' role has been ongoing. In addition to the Standards, which were drafted by the ASC, the Association's efforts are recorded in a number of documents. Among these are the ASC's *Academic Status: State-ments and Resources* of 1988[7] (soon to be reissued in an updated edition); the 1990 survey of faculty status reported by Lowry elsewhere in this volume; and the ASC-sponsored January 1992 think tank which produced "an agenda for strengthening faculty status for those institutions that have chosen that model for their librarians."[8]

In addition to faculty status, another option has attracted many academic librarians and institutions of higher education. This option is Academic Status: "an official recognition by an institution of postsecondary education that librarians are part of the instructional and research staff, but normally without entitlement to ranks and titles identical to those of faculty, and frequently without commensurate benefits, privileges, rights, and responsibilities."[9] The ASC also has been supportive of librarians who have or prefer academic status.[10]

The effect of the Standards on the lives of working librarians has been recorded in a large corpus of survey literature and the experiential reports on individual institutions.[11] This data traces an enduring commitment to faculty status among many librarians and a persistent gap between the Standards and the real environment of academic librarianship.

2. Views, opinions, advice, and recommendations.

The premise that "the academic librarian makes a unique and important contribution to American higher education"[12] never has been controversial. Whether "full" faculty status (as defined by the Standards) strengthens the library-university link and results in long-term improvement in library service, as those who favor faculty status assert, however, has been debated at length. The literature contains numerous examples of suggested alternatives to faculty status, proposed changes to the Standards, advice to librarians, opinion pieces, etc.

Academic status is the most widely practiced alternative to faculty status, and there are a number of writings that describe and advocate it.[13] Other alternatives include two-track systems in which librarians on one track are rewarded for service, research, etc. and those on a second track for administrative and supervisory accomplishment. Duda's description of the implementation of such a system at Columbia University[14] and Martin's advocacy of a dual system of "Professional Librarians" and "Occupational Librarians"[15] are examples. Batt advocates "optional faculty status."[16] Depew[17] proposes removal of the standards that require tenure and faculty rank for librarians. In 1979 Keys suggested librarians ally themselves with university administrators rather than faculty;[18] Gatten favors an alliance between academic and other librarians.[19] With the exception of academic status, none of these ideas has found strong acceptance among librarians or professional associations.

A common argument in opposition to faculty status is that the Standards do not fit "what librarians do" and that applying these conditions to academic librarians results in poor library service. This concern deserves attention. However, most writers who assert it make no attempt to describe what academic librarians' authority, responsibility, or core activities are or should be. Considering the many profound changes that have affected libraries, it is difficult to define librarians' professional work in any detail, but "what librarians do" when left too vague appears a fiat for an opinion about "what librarians should be doing."

The faculty status movement, which proposed profound changes in the professional lives of college and university librarians, has elicited strong emotional responses; and although undue optimism, outrage, and fear are less common than they were when faculty status was first proposed, high emotion is still present in status literature. Some early writings in favor of faculty status were sanguine, almost chauvinistic.[20] Anti-faculty status authors' passionate views range from those expressed with cogency, "As a library user, what do I expect of librarians? .... I want them available...not in a committee meeting or gone to a conference"[21] to histrionics, "I am an American first, a librarian second, and a cat-hater third. The faculty does its 'thing,' and I do mine."[22]

3. *Librarians and research.*

There is a considerable body of publication on librarian research,[23] such that, this topic alone deserves a literature review. Writers who favor faculty status and those who do not agree that this issue, more that any other, exemplifies librarians' ambiguous status.[24] "Faculty status has heightened the role conflict librarians experience between their commitment to library users and to scholarship,"[25] and librarians' dilemma--between scholarship requirements and lack of time, funds, and other support to do research--has been well-documented.[26]

4. *Social science applications.*

Studies that apply the methods of the social sciences--psychology, management, organizational behavior, etc.--to librarians have been published with some frequency. Earlier writings attempted to measure librarianship against social scientists' definitions of a profession in order to determine whether librarianship is a true profession.[27]

Current work is more sophisticated and applies research in career development, ergonomics, etc. to academic librarians. Kirkland, for example, based her study of librarians' difficulties with low status and ambiguous roles in psychology theory and methodology.[28] There also is a considerable literature on burnout[29] and plateauing,[30] which, while not applied specifically to faculty status, have been studied from the standpoint of librarians' career development. Mitchell and Morton's 1992 study of the professional acculturation of librarians offers insights that help account for the persistent emotional tone of faculty status writing.[31]

5. *Librarians as teachers.*

Shortly after the establishment of the Standards writers explored whether classroom teaching might be appropriate for library faculty.[32] This idea was opposed by writers who saw it as merely an attempt to "bolster a status claim."[33] At present teaching is generally agreed to be intrinsic to library service and has become embedded in library instruction programs; and, until very recently, there was less discussion of this issue.[34]

One recent article by a university administrator advocates librarians do more teaching partly to gain better understanding of traditional faculty.[35] Although there are a few recent instances of library faculty staffing high-enrollment classes (e.g., freshman English) as teacher of record, none of this has reached the literature; and nothing recent has been published on how many librarians do classroom teaching, what subjects they teach, or the advantages or disadvantages they and their colleagues see in this option.

Neglected topics

The themes above are only part of status literature, but all are significant in light of the current focus on the inseparability of the library and the university. Before discussing this trend, however, noting a few topics that are absent from status literature also can be instructive. The absence of the topics below exemplifies librarians' difficulty in adjusting to academe, as recently described by Mitchell and Morton.[36]

1. *The missing surveys.*

As noted above, surveys of librarians' opinions about status and actual conditions of work contain some of the most useful "hard" data in the literature. Most early surveys polled library directors, and there have been a number that queried university administrators. The trend to polling librarians themselves also began early and has continued, especially after being given impetus in 1983 by Davidson, Thorson, and Stine's "Faculty Status for Librarians: Querying the Troops."[37] Cook's 1981 survey of faculty at the University of Illinois, Carbondale[38] similarly inspired later surveys of faculty views of librarian performance.

Surveys of how librarians perceive the role and performance of faculty and university administrators in library programs, however, are wanting. Even the fairly-substantial collection development writings on the faculty role in building collections lack survey reports from a librarian perspective. Without doubt, librarians have strong, informed views on ideal and actual faculty and administrator relations with the library, but no poll of librarians on this question has been published.

2. *The relation between traditional faculty research and librarian research.*

Boice, Scepanski, and Wilson found that librarians and traditional faculty have similar styles of coping with pressures to publish.[39] Otherwise, very few writings on librarian research address commonalities and differences between librarians and faculty. Since the role of research in the university currently is being reexamined in both academe and the popular press,[40] examining librarian scholarship in isolation from the research environment in general is an especially unproductive and misleading approach.

3. *University service and its significance to libraries and librarians.*

Access to participation in university governance was the first standard to be widely realized by librarians with faculty and academic status.

Werrell and Sullivan reviewed writings pro and con on the place of governance and collegiality among librarians' responsibilities.[41] Other than Gamble's 1989 article pointing out the value of librarian service to the library's standing in the university community,[42] however, the kinds, extent, and level of librarian service and its significance for libraries and universities has received little attention.

Current trends and future prospects

Coming from a hierarchical, limited-autonomy tradition, librarians, even when seriously committed to faculty status as a goal, have not found the organization and communication styles of academe easy to master. Nevertheless, it is critical to the health of libraries and the institutions they serve that librarians play a strong role in the campus community, and librarians (with or without faculty status) still need to expend considerable effort before librarianship as a profession "swims" in the academic environment.

Early advocacy of faculty status for librarians can be traced in part to library directors' frustration with the poor treatment libraries received in comparison with that given high-status campus groups. Through succeeding decades, however, recognition of the importance of an intimate bond between librarians and their institutions has been no more than a thread through faculty status literature in comparison with the other themes mentioned in this chapter.[43] By the end of the 1980s an urgent note of fear that librarians may lose or give away their hard-won status[44] or become "isolated within the library"[45] entered faculty status writings.

Status literature has begun a change in focus away from debating faculty status, academic status, traditional status, etc. to emphasizing the acculturation necessary for librarians to gain autonomy and recognition and to contribute their increasingly special expertise to academe. The early 1990's brought new recognition that the integration of librarians and academe *is* critical, and writers now reprehend the "lack...of any relevant information concerning the librarian outside of the library and in the college or university where he/she works."[46] The January 1992 think tank is one expression of librarians' renewed emphasis on their role in institutions of higher education. In addition, a number of publications have appeared recently encouraging librarians to apply their expertise in larger settings via increased contact with faculty, students, and others. And writers in the 1990s are taking a new look at librarian service, research, etc. and offering ideas about how to realize a stronger librarian role via these activities.[47]

Conclusion

It is important that this new emphasis on the need for integration with academe also recognizes the real gains in professional growth many librarians have made in the decades since the establishment of the Standards.[48] However, the price that libraries and academe pay when librarians limit their purview to the library is a serious one. One of the basic tenets of administrative science and other disciplines concerned with the attributes of effective organizations is that responsibility without the authority (power) to exercise it is untenable, while professional autonomy plays a key role in organizational excellence.[49] Horenstein's study of job satisfaction among academic librarians found that "perception of participation appears to be the crucial factor....The best predictors of satisfaction were the extent to which the librarians perceive that they are involved in library planning and decision making,...informed about matters affecting the library, and in control of their own activities."[50] On any occasion that librarian expertise is disregarded and decisions on library programs are made outside the library, librarians suffer this responsibility-without-authority restraint. Fortunately administrators and faculty readily can recognize the destructiveness of this condition when it is called to their attention. But someone, preferably librarians who have forged strong links in their universities, must go out of the library and make this case.

Any academic librarian, with or without faculty status, can choose a more forceful and active role in his/her institution. Logically, this is so, but it would be irresponsible to claim that lack of faculty status does not make success in this more difficult. Faculty status offers points of access--service on university policy-making bodies, the opportunity to chair these bodies, the right to speak in faculty-only forums, joint appointments in teaching departments, etc.--that are unavailable under other status conditions. If these opportunities are taken, librarians can forge bonds of trust that can survive, even thrive, through everything from misunderstandings over library policies to massive journal cuts and new provosts' attempts to rescind librarians' tenure.

Oberg, Schleiter, and Van Houten identified a direct relation between the extent of faculty members' contact with librarians and their support for librarian tenure, faculty ranks, etc.[51] These findings credit the view that full membership in the campus community can breathe life into the Standards whose existence so often has seemed mainly on-paper and, thereby, advance librarians' progress out of "academic limbo."

---

1. For example, Arthur M. McAnally, "Status of the University Librarian in the Academic Community" in *Research Librarianship: Essays in Honor of Robert B. Downs*, ed. Jerrold Orne (New York: Bowker, 1971); Robert B. Downs, "The Role of the Academic Librarian, 1876-1976," *College & Research Libraries* 37 (Nov. 1976): 491-502; and Richard Hume Werking, "Allocating the Academic Library's Book Budget: Historical Perspectives and Current Reflections," *Journal of Academic Librarianship* 14 (1988): 140-44.

2. "Standards for Faculty Status for College and University Librarians," adopted by the membership of the Association of College and Research Libraries, Dallas, Texas, June 26, 1971, *College & Research Libraries News* 33 (Sept. 1972): 210-12; and American Library Association, Association of College and Research Libraries, Association of American Colleges, Association of American University Professors, "Statement on Faculty Status of College and University Librarians," *College & Research Libraries News* 35 (Feb. 1974): 26. See also, American Library Association, Association of College and Research Libraries, Academic Status Committee, "Standards for Faculty Status for College and University Librarians," revised version passed by ACRL Board of Directors on July 3, 1991, and approved by the ALA Standards Committee in January 1992, *College & Research Libraries News* 53 (May 1992): 317-18.

3. Janet Krompart, "Researching Faculty Status: A Selective Annotated Bibliography," *College & Research Libraries* 53 (Sept. 1992): 439

4. James F. Bailey and Mathew F. Dee, "Law School Libraries: Survey Relating to Autonomy and Faculty Status," *Law Library Journal* 67 (Feb. 1974): 17.

5. For example, Karl E. Johnson, *An Annotated Bibliography of Faculty Status in Library and Information Science* (Champaign, Ill.: Graduate School of Library and Information Science, Publications Office, University of Illinois at Urbana-Champaign, 1992): 3-4.

6. Krompart, "Researching Faculty Status."

7. American Library Association, Association of College and Research Libraries, Academic Status Committee, *Academic Status: Statements and Resources* (Chicago: ACRL, 1988).

8. Irene Hoadley, "Faculty Status: 2001," *College & Research Libraries News* 54 (June 1993): 338.

9. *ALA Glossary of Library and Information Science* (Chicago: ALA, 1983): 1.

10. American Library Association, Association of College and Research Libraries, Academic Status Committee, "ACRL Guidelines for Academic Status for College and University Libraries," *College & Research Libraries News* 51 (Mar. 1990): 245-46.

11. For a summary and update of survey results, see Janet Krompart and Clara DiFelice, "A Review of Faculty Status Surveys, 1971-1984," *Journal of Academic Librarianship* 13 (Mar. 1987): 14-18; Charles D. Lowry, "The Status of Faculty Status for Academic Librarians: A Twenty-Year Perspective," *College & Research Libraries* 54 (Mar.1993): 163-72. For reports of conditions at individual institutions, see, for example, Robert G. Sewell, "Faculty Status and Librarians: The Rationale and the Case of Illinois," *College & Research Libraries* 44 (May 1983): 212-22; and James L. Mullins, "Faculty Status of Librarians: A Comparative Study of Two Universities in the United Kingdom and How They Compare to the Association of College and Research Libraries Standards," in *Academic Librarianship Past, Present, and Future: A Festschrift in Honor of David Kaser*, ed. John Richardson, Jr. and Jinnie Y. Davis (Englewood, Colo.: Libraries Unlimited, 1989): 67-78.

12. "Standards for Faculty Status of College and University Librarians," adopted by the membership of the Association of College and Research Libraries, Dallas, Texas, June 26, 1971: 211.

13. For example, Joan M. Bechtel, "Academic Professional Status: An Alternative for Librarians," *Journal of Academic Librarianship* 11 (Nov. 1985): 289-92; and Malcomb P. Germann, Michael Kelly, and Rebecca Schreiner-Robles, "Faculty Status or Academic Status: Must We Choose?" paper read at the Fifth National Conference of the Association of College and Research Libraries, in *Building on the First Century* ed. Janice C. Fennell (Chicago: ACRL,1989): 15-18.

14. Frederick Duda, "Columbia's Two-Track System," *College & Research Libraries* 41 (July 1980): 295-304.

15. Susan Martin, "Raising Our Professional Expectations with a Two-Track Approach to Librarianship," *Journal of Academic Librarianship* 19 (1993): 24.

16. Fred Batt, "Faculty Status for Academic Librarians: Justified or Just a Farce?" in *Issues in Academic Librarianship: Views and Case Studies for the 1980s and 1990s*, ed. Peter Spyers-Duran and Thomas W. Mann, Jr. (Westport, Conn.: Greenwood, 1985): 115-28.

17. John N. DePew, "The ACRL Standards for Faculty Status: Panacea or Placebo," *College & Research Libraries* 44 (Nov. 1983): 407-13.

18. Marshall Keys, "Faculty Status: An Heretical View," *Mississippi Libraries* 43 (Summer 1979): 76-77.

19. Jeffrey N. Gatten, "Professionalism Revisited: Faculty Status and Academic Librarians," *Ohio Library Association Bulletin* 57 (Apr. 1987): 30-35.

20. For example, E. J. Josey, "Full Faculty Status This Century," *Library Journal* 97 (Mar. 15, 1972): 984-89.

21. Lawrence Clark Powell, "Shoe on the Other Foot: From Library Administrator to User," *Wilson Library Bulletin* 45 (Dec. 1970): 386.

22. Leslie R. Morris in a "Readers' Responses" letter appended to John Buschman, "The Real Issues of Faculty Status for Librarians," *Catholic Library World* 61 (Mar./Apr.1990): 222.

23. Emily Werrell and Laura Sullivan, "Faculty Status for Academic Librarians: A Review of the Literature," *College & Research Libraries* 48 (Mar.1987): 97-98.

24. For example, Gaby Divay and Carol Steer, "Academic Librarians Can Be Caught by the Pressure to Do Research," *Canadian Library Journal* 40 (Apr. 1983): 91-95.

25. Robert Boice, Jordan M. Scepanski, and Wayne Wilson. "Librarians and Faculty Members: Coping with Pressures to Publish," *College & Research Libraries* 48 (Nov. 1987): 494.

26. For example, Ronald Rayman and Frank Wm. Goudy, "Research and Publication Requirements in University Libraries," *College & Research Libraries* 41 (Jan. 1900): 43 48; and W. Bede Mitchell and L. Stanislava Swieszkowski, "Publication Requirements and Tenure Approval Rates: An Issue for Academic Librarians," *College & Research Libraries* 48 (Nov. 1987): 494-503.

27. For example, Mary Lee Bundy and Paul Wasserman, "Professionalism Reconsidered," *College & Research Libraries* 29 (Jan.1968): 5-26; and Gardner Hanks and C. James Schmidt, "An Alternative Model of a Profession for Librarians," *College & Research Libraries* 36 (May 1975): 175-87.

28. Janice J. Kirkland, "Equity and Entitlement: Internal Barriers to Improving the Pay of Academic Librarians," *College & Research Libraries* 52 (July1991). 375 80.

29. For example, Marcia J. Nauratil, *The Alienated Librarian* (New York: Greenwood, 1989).

30. For example, Mildred Merz, "Career Plateauing," *National Librarian* 13 (May 1988): 2-4.

31. W. Bede Mitchell and Bruce Morton, "On Becoming Faculty Librarians: Acculturation Problems and Remedies," *College & Research Libraries* 53 (Sept.1992): 379-92.

32. For example, Herman L. Totten, "A Survey of Academic Status of Black College and University Librarians," *Journal of Negro Education* 40 (Winter 1971): 342-46.

33. Pauline Wilson, "Librarians as Teachers: The Study of an Organization Fiction," *Library Quarterly* 49 (Apr. 1979): 146.

34. Werrell and Sullivan, "Faculty Status for Academic Librarians," 99-100.

35. W. Patrick Leonard, "More Librarians Should Consider Periodic Classroom Assignments," *Journal of Academic Librarianship* 15 (Mar. 1989): 28, 33.

36. Mitchell and Morton, "On Becoming Faculty Librarians."

37. Russ Davidson, Connie C. Thorson, and Diane Stine, "Faculty Status for Librarians: Querying the Troops," *College & Research Libraries* 44 (Nov. 1983): 415-20.

38. M. Kathy Cook, "Rank, Status, and Contribution of Academic Librarians as Perceived by the Teaching Faculty at Southern Illinois University, Carbondale," *College & Research Libraries* 42 (May 1981): 214-23.

39. Boice, Scepanski, and Wilson, "Librarians and Faculty Members."

40. For example, Charles J. Sykes, *Profscam: Professors and the Demise of Higher Education* (Washington, D.C.: St. Martin's, 1988); and Ernest L. Boyer, *Scholarship Reconsidered: Priorities of the Professoriate*, (Princeton, N.J.: Carnegie Foundation for the Advancement of Teaching, 1990).

41. Werrell and Sullivan, "Faculty Status for Academic Librarians," 98-99.

42. Lynne E. Gamble, "University Service: New Implications for Academic Librarians," *Journal of Academic Librarianship* 14 (Jan.1989): 344-47.

43. For example, Raleigh DePriest, "That Inordinate Passion for Status," *College & Research Libraries* 34 (Mar. 1973): 150-58; and Edward G. Holley, "Defining the Academic Librarian," *College & Research Libraries* 46 (Nov. 1985): 462-68.

44. For example, Gloriana St. Clair and Irene Hoadley, "The Challenge to Faculty Status: A Call to Militancy," *Wilson Library Bulletin* 63 (Dec. 1988): 23-24,26; and Gemma DeVinney and Mary L. Reichel, "Faculty Status: Lessons from the Past," paper read at the Fifth National Conference of the Association of College and Research Libraries, in *Building on the First Century*, ed. Janice C. Fennell (Chicago: ACRL, 1989): 12-14.

45. John Buschman, "The Flip Side of Faculty Status," *College & Research Libraries News* 50 (Dec.1989): 975.

46. H. Palmer Hall and Caroline Byrd, eds., *The Librarian in the University: Essays on Membership in the Academic Community* (Metuchen, N.J.: Scarecrow Press, 1990): 1.

47. For example, Hall and Bird, *The Librarian in the University* which has sections on university governance, teaching, research, and relations with students; Stephen E. Atkins, "Academic Librarians and the University," in his *The Academic Library in the American University* (Chicago: ALA, 1991): 159-88; Karyle Butcher, "Political Networking," *College & Research Libraries* 54 (July 1993): 291-92; and Gloriana St. Clair, "Elysian Thoughts on Librarians as Faculty," *College & Research Libraries* 54 (Jan. 1993): 7-9.

48. Beverley P. Lynch, in her review of Atkins, *The Academic Library in the American University*, criticizes Atkins's failure to acknowledge the successes librarians already have achieved in the turbulent "environments and political realities on most college and university campuses," *College & Research Libraries* 53 (Jan. 1992): 86.

49. For example, Thomas J. Peters and Robert H. Waterman, Jr., *In Search of Excellence: Lessons from America's Best-Run Companies* (New York: Harper and Row, 1982): 81.

50. Bonnie Horenstein, "Job Satisfaction of Academic Librarians: An Examination of the Relationships Between Satisfaction, Faculty Status, and Participation," *College & Research Libraries* 54 (May 1993): 264.

51. Larry R. Oberg , Mary Kay Schleiter, and Michael Van Houten, "Faculty Perceptions of Librarians at Albion College: Status, Role, Contribution, and Contacts," *College & Research Libraries* 50 (Mar. 1989): 215-30.

Researching Faculty Status:
A Selective Bibliography
Janet Krompart

Introduction

The literature of librarian status, faculty status in particular, has a long history of continuous publication that shows no sign of abating. In 1984, one writer recorded that "the literature of librarianship now contains hundreds of articles and several books on [this] subject . . . One conservative estimate, based on searches of *Library Literature, ERIC, DAI*, and Huling's (1973) [comprehensive] bibliography, places the figure well in excess of three hundred items."[1] Karl E. Johnson's 1992 comprehensive bibliography, which supplements Huling, contains more than 300 entries. He records a high of 219 faculty status titles published in the 1970's and more than 100 in the 1980's.[2]

Although this voluminous literature has been mapped by bibliographies and reviews, it remains time-consuming to master for either practical applications in libraries or further research. First of all, faculty status literature contains a variety of data and views. One writer has identified nine categories (bibliographies, surveys, position papers, etc.) into which it can be divided.[3] No matter how analysed, this literature includes at least four kinds of information:

1) a record of the Association of College and Research Libraries' long-term effort to establish a strong role for academic librarians;

2) the experiences of librarians who seek appropriate status in their institutions;

3) survey reports which quantify academic librarians' working conditions and views and record traditional faculty members' and others' assessments of librarians' contribution to academe; and

4) the views of those who support or oppose faculty status, advice to librarians, and other expressions of opinion.

In addition, faculty status is difficult to limit by subject. It is, in fact, not possible to determine the total number of faculty status publications because this topic is inseparable from related subjects: research, salary, and other contents of the nine standards, as well as academic status and wider issues regarding libraries, career development, women's professions, etc. While this characteristic may enrich and keep librarian faculty status in the wider contexts of academe and professionalism, it also precludes its containment as a subject.

Despite this diversity and the breadth of approaches which have been applied to status problems, these issues persistently defy resolution; and statements of frustration over librarians' undefined and under-recognized role also are common in the literature. Faculty status, as defined by the nine standards, has not been

Janet Krompart is Collection Development Coordinator at Oakland University Library, Rochester, Michigan.

realized fully; neither have writers who decry librarians' interest in faculty status proposed alternatives that attract much support.

In sum, faculty status literature is vast and diverse; its subject boundaries are indeterminate; and the issues it addresses remain unresolved. It is, nevertheless, the record of academic librarians' efforts to secure the authority their responsibilities require. Research and thought on status must continue and must be fortified by awareness of this history if librarians' right to make decisions about library programs is to be asserted successfully. The purpose of this bibliography is to help users of faculty status literature confidently apply its recorded experience to librarian status questions.

Coverage

This bibliography covers faculty status and, more selectively, its related subjects. It lists bibliographies and review articles, current and retrospective, and titles recommended as worth examining on the basis of these criteria:
1) has historical value; aids understanding of the background of status issues,
2) is frequently cited,
3) presents unique topics or innovative views or approaches, and
4) contains substantial references to publications of significance as described in 1-3.

Related subjects are represented in the bibliography, primarily by titles that are cited often or contain references equal to a basic bibliography of the subject.

Geographic coverage, generally, is limited to North America.

Arrangement

The bibliography has three sections:

A bibliography of bibliographies and reviews. The literature of faculty status is well-covered by bibliographies and review articles from its beginnings in the nineteenth century to the present, and bibliographers have taken reasonable care to assure full coverage.

The large, general bibliographies that substantially cover faculty status literature are: Huling (No. 4), coverage through 1973; Johnson (No. 5), 1974-1991; and Werrell and Sullivan (No. 8), selective coverage, 1974-1985. Annotations of titles in this bibliography which also are cited by any of these large bibliographies are followed by H, J, or W.

Selective recent publications, 1985-1992. Titles in this section aid understanding of status issues (Criterion 1), introduce new perspectives (Criterion 3), or contain useful references (Criterion 4). In addition, this section includes recent notable faculty status titles that do not appear in other bibliographies.

Early, frequently-cited titles, published through 1985. Titles that have historical value or are frequently cited (Criteria 1 and 2).

Abbreviations

ACRL Standards—Standards for Faculty Status for College and University Librarians, 1971 (No. 51) and 1992 (No. 12)

H—cited in N. Huling's bibliography (No. 4)

J—cited in K. Johnson's bibliography (No. 5)

W—cited in E. Werrell and L. Sullivan's bibliography (No. 8)

Definitions

"Academic Status." *ALA Glossary of Library and Information Science.* Ed. Heartsill Young. Chicago: ALA, 1983. 1.

"An official recognition by an institution of postsecondary education that librarians are part of the instructional and research staff, but normally without entitlement to ranks and titles identical to those of faculty, and frequently without commensurate benefits, privileges, rights, and responsibilities."

"Faculty Status." *ALA Glossary of Library and Information Science.* Ed. Heartsill Young. Chicago: ALA, 1983. 9.

"An official recognition by an institution of postsecondary education that librarians are part of the instructional and research staff by conferment of ranks and titles identical to those of faculty, and commensurate benefits, privileges, rights, and responsibilities."

Sources

This bibliography grew from the interest of the Academic Status Committee, Association of College and Research Libraries, in facilitating association members' use of faculty status literature. The committee has a "consulting role in working with individuals or groups in addressing faculty status issues in individual institutions,"[4] and is mindful of the need, sometimes urgent, for academic librarians to be aware of librarian status documents and other materials.

The basic sources examined in the preparation of the bibliography are those traditionally consulted by researchers and bibliographers in librarianship and information science: *Dissertation Abstracts International, ERIC, LISA,* and *Library Literature.* In addition, browsing in the Information and Library Studies Library, University of Michigan, revealed useful unindexed items. Familiarity with faculty status literature developed during an examination of faculty status surveys[5] and making and re-making the case for full faculty status for librarians at Oakland University[6] also supported this project.

1. Patricia Ohl Rice, *Academic Freedom and Faculty Status for Academic Librarians: A Bibliographical Essay* ERIC, ED 246 917, 1984, p.5.

2. Karl E. Johnson, *An Annotated Bibliography of Faculty Status* (Champaign, IL: Graduate School of Library and Information Science, Publications Office, University of Illinois at Urbana-Champaign, 1992).

3. Batt, Fred, "Faculty Status for Academic Librarians: Justified or Just a Farce?" *Issues in Academic Librarianship: Views and Case Studies for the 1980s and 1990s* Ed. Peter Spyers Duran and Thomas W. Mann, Jr. (Westport, CT: Greenwood, 1985), p.115-128.

4. American Library Association. Association of College and Research Libraries. Committee on Academic Status, *Academic Status: Statements and Resources* (Chicago: ALA, 1988), iii.

5. Janet Krompart and Clara DiFelice, "A Review of Faculty Status Surveys, 1971-1984," *Journal of Academic Librarianship* 13:14-18 (March 1987).

6. Janet Krompart and Richard L. Pettengill, "Eight-month Contracts for Oakland University Librarians," *College and Research Libraries News* 51: 976-978 (November 1990).

A bibliography of bibliographies and reviews

1. Batt, Fred. "Faculty Status for Academic Librarians: Justified or Just a Farce?" *Issues in Academic Librarianship: Views and Case Studies for the 1980s and 1990s.* Ed. Peter Spyers-Duran and Thomas W. Mann, Jr. Westport, CT: Greenwood, 1985. 115-128.
Reviews faculty status literature dividing the topic into nine categories that include bibliographies, surveys, and policies; analyses by geography, institution, etc.; broader topics in academe; subtopics of faculty status; and position papers. "Optional faculty status" for individual librarians is an alternative to "force-fitting" librarians into the faculty mold. 40 notes. J

2. DeBoer, Kee, and Wendy Culotta. "The Academic Librarian and Faculty Status in the 1980s: A Survey of the Literature." *College and Research Libraries* 48 (May 1987): 215-223. Reprinted in *Academic Status: Statements and Resources* (No. 9).
A "composite profile of the current academic librarian" as reflected in the literature. Topics covered include faculty versus academic status, tenure and other provisions of the ACRL Standards, publishing pressure and productivity. 97 notes. J

3. Harring, Mark Y. "A Race Between Education and Catastrophe: The MLS and Beyond: Tenure and Faculty Status." *Controversial Issues in Librarianship: An Annotated Bibliography, 1960-1984.* New York: Garland, 1987. 282-286.
A selective list of 20 journal articles on various aspects of faculty status. Nine of these articles, mostly dating from the late 1970s, make forceful arguments pro and con.

4. Huling, Nancy. "Faculty Status: A Comprehensive Bibliography." *College and Research Libraries* 34 (November 1973): 440-462.
The basic annotated bibliography of librarian faculty status, 1878-1973. Lists 218 titles. Supplemented by Werrell (No.8) and by Johnson (No. 5). J

5. Johnson, Karl E. *An Annotated Bibliography of Faculty Status in Library and Information Science.* University of Illinois, Graduate School of Library and Information Science. Occasional Papers 193. Champaign, IL: Graduate School of Library and Information Science, Publications Office, University of Illinois at Urbana-Champaign, 1992. 66 pp.
A supplement to Huling (No. 4). This comprehensive bibliography cites over 300 English-language items published 1973-1991, including a few pre-1973 titles not listed by

Huling. Each citation is followed the original abstract or a brief annotation.

6. Krompart, Janet, and Clara DiFelice. "A Review of Faculty Status Surveys, 1971-1984." *Journal of Academic Librarianship* 13 (March 1987): 14-18. Reprinted in *Academic Status: Statements and Resources* (No. 9).
A review of 36 surveys published since establishment of the ACRL Standards 1971. The surveys document disparity and confusion between stated goals of the profession and actual circumstances of librarians. 20 notes. J

7. Werrell, Emily, and Laura Sullivan. "Faculty Status for Academic Librarians: A Review of the Literature." *College and Research Libraries* 48 (March 1987): 95-103. Reprinted in *Academic Status: Statements and Resources* (No. 9).
Summarizes trends in opinions about faculty status in the literature, 1974-1987. Also reviews writings on publication/scholarship, governance and collegiality, librarians as teachers, and collective bargaining. 56 notes. J

8. ———. *Faculty Status for Academic Librarians: An Annotated Bibliography.* 1985. ERIC, ED 274 364. 57 pp.
A selective list of 121 titles, 1974-1985. "General or view pieces on faculty status or an aspect of it." Supplements Huling (No. 4) and is supplemented by Johnson (No. 5). J

Selective recent publications, 1985-1992

9. American Library Association. Association of College and Research Libraries. Academic Status Committee. *Academic Status: Statements and Resources.* Chicago: ACRL, 1988. 58 pp.
A collection that contains the ACRL Standards 1971 (No. 51), other standards and guidelines related to faculty status, reprints of review articles on faculty status (Nos. 2, 6, and 7), and a select bibliography of 44 titles. J

10. ———. "ACRL Guidelines for Academic Status for College and University Libraries." *College and Research Libraries News* 51 (March 1990): 245-246.
Nine guidelines for "institutions which have not yet achieved faculty rank, status, and tenure for academic librarians." Approved by the ACRL Board at the Midwinter Meeting 1990. J

11. ———. "ACRL Standards for Faculty Status for College and University Librarians: A Draft Revision." *College and Research Libraries News* 51 (May 1990): 402-404.
Discusses Academic Status Committee plans for revision of the ACRL Standards 1971 and invites those interested in influencing the reformulation of this draft revision of the ACRL Standards to attend a 1990 (ALA, Chicago) hearing or contact the ASC directly.

12. ———. "Standards for Faculty Status for College and University Librarians." *College and Research Libraries News* 53 (May 1992): 317-318.
The revised version of the ACRL Standards 1971 passed by the ACRL Board of Directors, July 3, 1991 and approved by the ALA Standards Committee, January 1992. Prefatory material presents rationale and history of

this revision. Compare No. 51, ACRL Standards 1971.

13. Arlen, Shelley, and Nedria Santizo. "Administrative Support for Research: A Survey of Library Faculty." *Library Administration and Management* 4 (Fall 1990): 208-212.
A report on 56 surveys on release time and other support for research received by librarians with faculty status in 37 ARL libraries. Librarian scholarship is poorly supported, but there is a trend to repair this lack. This support is especially important for untenured librarians whose hire and training represent a considerable cost to the institution. 20 notes.

14. Atkins, Stephen E. "Academic Librarians and the University." *The Academic Library in the American University*. Chicago: ALA, 1991. 159-188.
Discusses problems facing academic librarians (technological change, difficult clientele, teaching and research demands, etc.). The major adjustment librarians must make is to increase their understanding of academe and the politics of working with traditional faculty and other elements of their university. 142 notes.

15. Benedict, Marjorie A. "Librarians' Satisfaction with Faculty Status." *College and Research Libraries* 52 (November 1991): 538-548.
Results two of surveys of opinion (1982 and 1989) on faculty status conducted among librarians in eight institutions of the State University of New York system. *Academic* faculty status was preferred, but sentiment for *equitable* faculty status was also strong. Satisfaction was greater where conditions conformed to the ACRL Standards. 8 notes. J

16. Blake, Fay M. "In the Eye of the Storm: Academic Librarianship in the Sixties." *Activism in American Librarianship, 1962-1973*. Ed. Mary Lee Bundy and Frederick J. Stielow. New York: Greenwood, 1987. 61-72.
Describes librarians' traditional "handmaiden's" role, the recognition of the need for change which flourished with the social unrest of the 1960s, and improvements made in librarians' status at the University of California at Los Angeles. 17 notes.

17. Boice, Robert, Jordan M. Scepanski, and Wayne Wilson. "Librarians and Faculty Members: Coping with Pressures to Publish." *College and Research Libraries* 48 (November 1987): 494-503.
A study of librarians and traditional faculty, done by a professor of psychology. The two groups' competence and approaches to research and publication are similar. Both need to improve effectiveness of their use of time. 18 notes. J

18. Brody, Catherine T. "Faculty Status for Academic Librarians: The Dream and the Reality." *Bookmark* 45 (Fall 1986): 42-47. ERIC, ED 287 479. 5 pp.
The perspective of a library director (New York City Technical College, City University of New York). Reports CUNY's experience with faculty status and calls for librarians to increase activity in their profession

and to improve communication with university administrators and others in their institutions. J

19. Cain, Mark E. "Academic and Research Librarians: Who Are We?" *Journal of Academic Librarianship* 14 (November 1988): 292-296.
A demographic report: age, year of library degree, sex, geographic location, education, and language and professional skills of a 1986 sampling of 1,771 academic and research librarians in North America. Included here as useful information for faculty status research projects. 2 notes.

20. Clinefelter, Ruth W., and Jack E. Hibbs. "The Neglected Information Specialist." *Academe* 75 (July-August 1989): 26-30.
Discusses barriers to salary equity between academic librarians and traditional faculty in terms of the uneven progress in realization of the ACRL Standards. 6 notes.

21. D'Amicantonio, John. *Evaluating Library Faculty*. 1989. ERIC, ED 311 787. 9 pp.
Describes modifications made by librarians to the California State University at Long Beach faculty retention, tenure, and promotion document. These changes included adding descriptions of librarian skills criteria. Peer review and other sections appropriate to librarians were not changed. 8 notes.

22. DeVinney, Gemma. "Academic Librarians and Academic Freedom in the United States: A History and Analysis." *Libri* 36 (1986): 24-39.

Traces the history of academic freedom and compares its application to traditional faculty and librarians. Academic freedom for librarians largely has had an intellectual freedom model, which focuses on library users' right to information, while the professional model for other faculty is centered on professional status. 74 notes. J

23. ———. "The 1965-1974 Faculty Status Movement As a Professionalization Effort with Social Movement Characteristics: A Case Study of the State University of New York." Diss. State U of New York at Buffalo, 1987. 332 pp.
State University of New York librarians made intense efforts to achieve full faculty status during the period 1965-1974. Their activities during these years included lobbying for academic ranks, establishing the SUNY Library Association, and participating in collective bargaining. Not seen; annotation based on *Dissertation Abstracts International* 48 (1988): 2481A.

24. DeVinney, Gemma, and Mary L. Reichel. "Faculty Status: Lessons from the Past." *Building on the First Century*. Proc. of the Fifth National Conference of the Association of College and Research Libraries. Cincinnati, 5-8 April 1989. Ed. Janice C. Fennell. Chicago: ACRL, 1989. 12-14.
Expresses concern that librarians may forget the history of faculty status and become willing to relinquish gains, such as, access to academic promotions. Proposes an oral history project of interviews with pioneers of faculty status and a faculty status think tank to identify a future agenda. 11 notes.

25. Gamble, Lynne E. "University Service: New Implications for Academic Librarians." *Journal of Academic Librarianship* 14 (January 1989): 344-347.
Emphasizes the critical importance of university service for academic libraries and librarians, using the California State University system as an example. Faculty status has opened the door to a librarian role in governance. 15 notes. J

26. Gatten, Jeffrey N. "Professionalism Revisited: Faculty Status and Academic Librarians." *Ohio Library Association Bulletin* 57 (April 1987): 30-51.
Opposes faculty status. Librarians should ally themselves with librarians in a unified profession instead of "declaring allegiance to the teaching faculty." 9 notes. J

27. Germann, Malcolm P., Michael Kelly, and Rebecca Schreiner-Robles. "Faculty Status or Academic Status: Must We Choose?" *Building on the First Century*. Proc. of the Fifth National Conference of the Association of College and Research Libraries. Cincinnati, 5-8 April 1989. Ed. Janice C. Fennell. Chicago: ACRL, 1989. 15-18.
Librarians at Wichita State University have kept faculty status but revised their tenure and promotion document to incorporate features of academic status. 2 notes. Copy of rev. document appended. J

28. Hall, H. Palmer, and Caroline Byrd, eds. *The Librarian in the University: Essays on Membership in the Academic Community*. Metuchen, NJ: Scarecrow, 1990. 199 pp.
A collection of 18 essays under the categories "The Librarian in University Governance" (7), "The Librarian as Teacher" (4), "Research, Publication and networking..." (3), and The Librarian and the Student..." (4), and a bibliographical essay which offers a starting point for librarians and other faculty to inform themselves about university participation beyond their libraries and academic units.

29. Heruhel, Jean-Pierre V. M. "To 'Degree' or not to 'Degree': Academic Librarians and Subject Expertise." *College and Research Libraries News* 52 (July/August 1991): 437.
A brief position paper that explores the pros and cons of additional graduate degrees for librarians. "Librarians should undergo this rite of passage" which enlarges their skills and contribution to academe. 2 notes.

30. Hill, Fred E., and Robert Hauptman. "A New Perspective on Faculty Status." *College and Research Libraries* 47 (March 1986): 156-159.
A study of whether librarians deserve faculty status, done following a random survey of librarians which showed faculty status continues as an important issue. Similarities between librarians and medical school faculty are worth investigating to determine the most appropriate model for librarians. Only librarians who teach, research, and publish should have faculty status. 9 notes. J

31. Jackson, Joseph A., and R. Wilburn Clouse. "Academic Library Status: A Review of Employment Opportunities." *Behavioral and Social Sciences Librarian* 6.3/4 (1988): 139-166.

A study of 527 Chronicle of Higher Education advertisements for librarian positions that covers some of the ACRL Standards: ranks, calendar, research, etc. Academic rank and tenure, research and publication requirements, and the 12-month calendar are among the common features of these advertisements. 13 notes. J

32. Kellogg, Rebecca. "Faculty Members and Academic Librarians: Distinctive Differences." *College and Research Libraries News* 48 (November 1987): 602-606.
Observations of an administrator (Associate Dean, College of Arts and Sciences, University of Arizona), who is also a librarian, regarding administrators' views of librarians and traditional faculty. Librarians should set aside the status question and focus on communicating librarians' unique knowledge and their contributions to institutional goals. J

33. Kirkland, Janice J. "Equity and Entitlement: Internal Barriers to Improving the Pay of Academic Librarians." *College and Research Libraries* 52 (July 1991): 375-380.
Social and psychological research data is apt for understanding librarians' psychological barriers to attaining the rewards they deserve and for identifying the skills they need to gain equitable salaries. 16 notes.

34. Lawson, V. Lonnie. "Faculty Status of Academic Librarians in Missouri." *Show-Me Libraries* 38 (June 1987): 3-8.
A survey of ten public university library directors in Missouri which asks about the status of librarians at these schools and the directors' opinions of faculty status. Whether faculty status is "contrived status" for librarians remains a debated question. 4 notes; bibliography of 8 items.

35. Leonard, W. Patrick. "On My Mind: More Librarians Should Consider Periodic Classroom Assignments." *Journal of Academic Librarianship* 15 (March 1989): 28, 33.
Leonard, Vice Chancellor for Academic Services, Purdue University, Westville IN, feels that, local conditions permitting, librarians should engage in classroom teaching. The benefits include ameliorating librarian isolation from mainstream teaching and learning. J

36. Meyer, Richard W. "Earnings Gains through the Institutionalized Standard of Faculty Status." *Library Administration and Management* 4 (Fall 1990): 184-193.
An application of economic theory and methodology to salary and other data for librarians and faculty at Clemson and 15 other universities. Faculty status raises librarian salaries collectively, but institutional productivity (i.e., doctoral degrees to total degrees granted, used here as a simple proxy) is lower where librarian publication rates are high. 23 notes.

37. Mitchell, Wilfrid Bede. "Faculty Status for Academic Librarians: Compliance with Standards, Opinions of University Administrators, and a Comparison of Tenure-Success Records of Librarians and Instructional Faculty." Diss. Montana State U, 1989. 173 pp.

Reports a mail/telephone survey of academic administrators, library directors, and librarians active in the faculty status movement "to determine whether certain concerns about librarian faculty status are justified." Among the findings: there is no trend to or from application of the ACRL Standards; librarian and other faculty tenure rates are similar; most administrators favor an alternative to the Standards. Not seen: annotation based on *Dissertation Abstracts International* 50 (1990): 1827A.

38. Mullins, James L. "Faculty Status of Librarians: A Comparative Study of Two Universities in the United Kingdom and How They Compare to the Association of College and Research Libraries Standards." *Academic Librarianship Past, Present, and Future: A Festschrift in Honor of David Kaser*. Ed. John Richardson, Jr. and Jinnie Y. Davis. Englewood, CO: Libraries Unlimited, 1989. 67-78.
Case studies of Oxford University and the University of Bristol conducted to determine to what extent their librarians' status fits criteria that parallel the ACRL Standards. Status for British librarians is less well defined, but their circumstances are similar to those of U.S. librarians. 29 notes.

39. Oberg, Larry R., Mary Kay Schleiter, and Michael Van Houten. "Faculty Perceptions of Librarians at Albion College: Status, Role, Contribution, and Contacts." *College and Research Libraries* 50 (March 1989): 215-230.
A survey of Albion faculty asked for views of librarians' status, role, and

contribution. Among the findings: faculty often do not distinguish librarians from support staff but the greater faculty contact with librarians the greater their support for librarians' tenure, faculty rank, etc. 30 notes. Copy of survey questionnaire included. J

40. Olevnik, Peter P. *A Study of the Organizational Implications of Faculty Status for Librarians in the College Library*. 1986. ERIC, ED 270 121. 24 pp.
A report on 235 responses to a random survey of directors in public and independent institutions with centralized and decentralized libraries and varying sizes of librarian staffs. Neither faculty status nor lack of it showed strong relation to organization structures, and faculty status was not more common in either bureaucratic or collegial organizations. 7 notes. J

41. Page, Jacqueline Marie. "The Pursuit of Professional Identity for Librarianship Within American Higher Education: A Study of Educational Programs and Work Requirements in Socialization for Academic Identity in the 1980s." Diss. Saint Louis U, 1990. 485 pp.
Exploration of the hypothesis that librarians are insufficiently enculturated to being faculty. A literature review and content analyses of library school catalogs and position advertisements demonstrated the lack of systematic preparation for this role. Not seen: annotation based on *Dissertation Abstracts International* 52 (1991): 10A.

42. Park, Betsy, and Robert Riggs. "Status of the Profession: A 1989

National Survey of Tenure and Promotion Policies for Academic Librarians." *College and Research Libraries* 52 (May 1991): 275-289.

A 1989 survey which yielded 304 responses from randomly-selected academic libraries. The continued primacy of job performance as an evaluation factor and widespread emphasis on service in comparison with research are among the findings. Includes a review of the literature. 40 notes. J

43. Parker, Diane C. "Librarians: An Element of Diversity within the Faculty." *College and Research Libraries News* 50 (September 1989): 675-677.

A succinct answer to the question "Why are librarians faculty?" presented by a library director (Western Washington University). Lists fundamental similarities and differences of the two groups and concludes that they collaborate closely and are equally important to the academic enterprise. J

44. St. Clair, Gloriana, and Irene Hoadley. "The Challenge to Faculty Status: A Call to Militancy." 63 *Wilson Library Bulletin* (December 1988): 23-24, 26.

Describes challenge to faculty status at Texas A&M University when a new provost was installed in 1986, how that crisis was met by librarians, and some positive results from the experience. J

45. Schwartz, Charles A. "Research Productivity and Publication Output: An Interdisciplinary Analysis." *College and Research Libraries* 52 (September 1991): 414-424.

An examination of library science research productivity. Several factors (e.g., available time) are less significant than often assumed. Suggests new perspectives on the study of librarian productivity. 54 notes.

46. Simon, Matthew J. "The Library Director's Role in Colleges and Universities Where Librarians Are Faculty." *Urban Academic Librarian* 5 (Fall 1987): 20-30.

Faculty status for librarians places library directors in the position of balancing librarians' expectations with those of the university administration. Among the ways directors can maximize faculty benefits are commissioning in-house research projects and redefining assignments to exclude clerical tasks. 15 notes. J

47. Smith, John Brewster. "Faculty Status of Librarians in Three ARL Member Research Libraries in New York State: A Case Study." Diss. Columbia U, 1991. 369pp.

A multi-faceted study of faculty status at three New York State ARL libraries which includes surveys of governance leaders and administrators, an examination of governance documents, and on-site visits by the investigator. Among the findings: librarians prefer faculty status but are ambivalent about some aspects of it, e.g., practical problems in the application of personnel review criteria. Not seen: annotation based on *Dissertation Abstracts International* 52 (1992): 2743A.

48. Turner, Bonnie L., and Ellen I. Watson. *Promotion and Tenure for Library Faculty*. 1989. ERIC, ED 331 504. 7 pp.

An example of an internal document (Bradley University) that makes a case for faculty status for academic librarians on the basis of the ACRL Standards and establishes criteria for tenure and promotion of library faculty.

49. Walden, Winston Allen. "Academic Status of Librarians in State-Supported Nondoctorate-Granting, Four-Year Colleges and Universities (Faculty)." Diss. Southern Illinois U at Carbondale, 1985. 471 pp.
A report of a survey of 284 libraries' compliance with the ACRL Standards which presents the percentage of libraries in full compliance with each standard. Few libraries met all nine fully, but librarians' rights and responsibilities were found similar to those of other faculty, and library faculty are more likely to work under Standards conditions than librarians not considered faculty. Not seen: annotation based on *Dissertation Abstracts International* 47 (1986): 698A.

50. Winter, Michael F. *The Culture and Control of Expertise: Toward a Sociological Understanding of Librarianship.* New York: Greenwood, 1988. 154 pp.
Application of particular sociological theories to the question of whether librarianship is a profession is too limited. Wider exploration of sociological research (studies of professions and occupations, issues of autonomy and control, etc.) can lead librarians to think about their work in new ways.

Early, frequently-cited titles published through 1985
51. American Library Association. Association of College and Research Libraries. "Standards for Faculty Status for College and University Librarians." *College and Research Libraries News* 33 (September 1972): 210-212 and 35 (May 1974): 112-113. Reprinted in *Academic Status: Statements and Resources* (No. 9). Compare No. 12, ACRL Standards 1992. The nine standards that "recognize formally the college or university librarian's academic status," adopted by the ACRL membership in Dallas, TX on June 26, 1971. H

52. ————. Academic Status Committee. *Faculty Status for Academic Librarians: A History and Policy Statements.* Chicago: ALA, 1975. 55 pp.
A compilation of basic faculty status documents and a reprint of a key article on the historical development of faculty status (No. 66). J W

53. Association of Research Libraries. Office of Management Services. SPEC Kit, 61. *The Status of Librarians: An Overview.* Washington, DC: ARL, OMS, February 1980. 105 pp.
A 1979 survey of ARL libraries: type of status, promotion, tenure, and other benefits equivalent to those of traditional faculty. Results are reported on a copy of the questionnaire. Documents on appointment, promotion and tenure, ranking structure, etc. of 11 universities are included. J W

54. Bailey, Martha J. "Some Effects of Faculty Status on Supervision in Academic Libraries." *College and Research Libraries* 37 (January 1976): 48-52.
Faculty status makes the competition among librarians' major commitments

(exportion, administration, and professional status) so acute that these conflicting responsibilities become detrimental to academic library management. 12 notes. J W

55. Bechtel, Joan M. "Academic Professional Status: An Alternative for Librarians." *Journal of Academic Librarianship* 11 (November 1985): 289-292.
Since 1981 Dickinson College librarians and other academic support personnel have had the title "academic professional " For Dickinson librarians, formerly out of contact with faculty and "horrified at the notion of service on committees" or teaching, academic professional status has provided clear responsibilities and improved rewards. 2 notes. J W

56. Bentley, Stella. "Collective Bargaining and Faculty Status." *Journal of Academic Librarianship* 4 (1978): 75-81.
Reports on a survey of librarians at six libraries, three with collective bargaining. Librarians without a bargaining agent are more likely to have to meet scholarship criteria without the necessary time and money to do so; and those with collective bargaining tend to be less satisfied with their economic status. 8 notes. J W

57. Branscomb, Lewis C., ed. *The Case for Faculty Status for Academic Librarians.* ACRL Monograph, no. 33. Chicago: ALA, 1970. 122 pp.
Fifteen papers in support of faculty status by Robert B. Downs, Arthur M. McAnally, David C. Weber, and others associated with the ACRL Ad Hoc

Committee on Academic Status, 1958-1960. Historic statements of the views that led to adoption of the ACRL Standards. H

58. Cook, M. Kathy. "Rank, Status, and Contribution of Academic Librarians as Perceived by the Teaching Faculty at Southern Illinois University, Carbondale." *College and Research Libraries* 42 (May 1981): 214-223.
A survey of teaching faculty views on librarians' contribution to teaching and research. More than half the respondents favored faculty status for librarians. Many saw professorial ranks as inseparable from research, but many also felt librarians should resolve the research issue themselves. Copy of survey questionnaire included. 8 Notes. J W

59. DePew, John N. "The ACRL Standards for Faculty Status: Panacea or Placebo." *College and Research Libraries* 44 (November 1983): 407-413.
A proposal to achieve an appropriate and attainable standard for librarians by modifying ACRL Standards five and six (tenure and faculty rank). Librarian, not faculty, status would help librarians to their goal of providing better library service. 23 notes. J W

60. DePriest, Raleigh. "That Inordinate Passion for Status." *College and Research Libraries* 34 (March 1973): 150-158.
Analyzes the anti-faculty status arguments of Kenneth Kister, Daniel Gore, Lawrence Clark Powell, and others. Librarians desire for status is serious and not "inordinate" because of their professional responsibility to maintain

the library and resist detrimental political pressures. 21 notes. H

61. Divay, Gaby, and Carol Steer. "Academic Librarians Can Be Caught by the Pressure to Do Research." *Canadian Library Journal* 40 (April 1983): 91-95.
A research requirement is not apt for librarians. Some reasons: librarians are not employed to teach or do research and they have less need to keep up with research trends in their field, which is technical rather than subject oriented. If research is required, institutions must allow librarians to meet this requirement in realistic terms. 18 notes; bibliography of 32 items. J W

62. Downs, Robert B., ed. *The Status of American College and University Librarians*. ACRL Monograph, no. 22. Chicago: ALA, 1958. 176 pp.
A collection of papers by Downs, Patricia B. Knapp, Arthur M. McAnally, and others published to provide "practical assistance to librarians and institutions struggling with matters of status." Includes studies of librarians' circumstances and views on faculty status, discussions of librarians' role, descriptions of personnel programs at specific institutions, etc. H

63. English, Thomas G. "Librarian Status in the Eighty-Nine U.S. Academic Institutions of the Association of Research Libraries: 1982." *College and Research Libraries* 44 (May 1983): 199-211.
A detailed presentation of the results of a 1982 faculty status survey of the 89 ARL libraries. Over 60 percent of state-supported institutions grant faculty status to librarians, but the trend to faculty status seems to have slowed and, to some extent, reversed. 11 notes. J W

64. Josey, E. J. "Full Faculty Status This Century: The Report of a Survey of new York State Academic Libraries." *Library Journal* 97 (15 March 1972): 984-989.
A survey of New York State academic librarians' attitudes to faculty status and the ACRL Standards. Ninety percent saw themselves as faculty, but librarians must struggle for status and institutions of higher education must respond positively to make it a reality by the 21st century. 8 notes. H

65. Keys, Marshall. "Faculty Status: An Heretical View." *Mississippi Libraries* 43 (Summer 1979): 76-77.
Librarians' affinity is to other administrators. It is librarians' unique ability to deliver information that is worthy of respect. Emulation of faculty is a futile search for "false gods" and "illusory ends." J W

66. McAnally, Arthur M. "Status of the University Librarian in the Academic Community." Ed. Jerrold Orne. *Research Librarianship: Essays in Honor of Robert B. Downs*. New York: Bowker, 1971. 19-50. Reprinted in *Faculty Status for Academic Librarians: A History and Policy Statements* (No. 52).
A brief history of academic librarianship from the late 19th century to 1970. The prognosis for acceptance of faculty status is good; and projections of how librarians' educational role, changes in library organi-

zation, application of academic freedom and tenure to librarians, etc. might work out indicate that faculty status is feasible for librarians. 60 notes. H

67. Mason, Ellsworth. "A Short Happy View of Our Emulation of Faculty." *College and Research Libraries* 33 (November 1972): 445-446.
Opposes faculty status on the ground that librarians have more to lose (e.g., freedom from "publish-or-perish") than to gain. The most important goals (high regard for the library and attraction and retention of excellent librarians) can be achieved without faculty status. H

68. Massman, Virgil F. *Faculty Status for Librarians.* Metuchen, NJ: Scarecrow, 1972. 229 pp.
A review of faculty status literature and a report on surveys of librarians and traditional faculty at 19 state institutions of higher education in three midwestern states. The surveys compared education, professional activities, working conditions, etc. of librarians and faculty. Faculty status is essential for full librarian participation in academe. H

69. Mitchell, W. Bede, and L. Stanislava Swieszkowski. "Publication Requirements and Tenure Approval Rates: An Issue for Academic Librarians." *College and Research Libraries* 46 (May 1985): 249-255.
A report of a survey of 189 Center for Research Libraries academic library members (94.5% return) on research and publication requirements for librarian tenure. The most frequent cause of denial of librarian tenure is

insufficient research, but the librarian tenure rate (81.5%) is higher than that of traditional faculty (58%). Copy of survey questionnaire included. 10 notes. J W

70. Powell, Lawrence Clark. "Shoe on the Other Foot: From Library Administrator to User." *Wilson Library Bulletin* 45 (December 1970): 384-389.
A post-retirement personal and experiential view of librarianship by the former Dean of the University of California at Los Angeles Graduate School of Library Service. Higher status for librarians must come from what librarians do; if they do what faculty do they are faculty, not librarians. Librarians gain status by hard work and study of their own field.

71. Query, Lance. "Librarians and Teaching Faculty: Disparity within the System." *Academe* 71 (July-August 1985): 13-16.
Reviews salary inequity and the failure of faculty and administrators to recognize librarians' unique role. No matter what type of formal status librarians have, they have second-class faculty status in terms of salary. J W

72. Rayman, Ronald, and Frank Wm. Goudy. "Research and Publication Requirements in University Libraries." *College and Research Libraries* 41 (January 1980): 43-48.
A report on a survey of 94 ARL libraries regarding academic librarian research and publication. Fifteen percent of these libraries require librarian research and publication for favorable reviews. Whatever the re-

quirement, however, librarian research is not well-supported. 11 notes. J

73. Rice, Patricia Ohl. *Academic Freedom and Faculty Status for Academic Librarians: A Bibliographical Essay.* 1984. ERIC, ED 246 917. 18 pp.
A review of 13 publications (1956-1975) which give academic freedom as a rationale for librarian faculty status. The infrequent use of this argument by librarians probably is due to the ambiguity of the term academic freedom and to librarians' confusing it with intellectual freedom. 4 notes; 9 added references. J W

74. Sewell, Robert G. "Faculty Status and Librarians: The Rationale and the Case of Illinois." *College and Research Libraries* 44 (May 1983): 212-222.
The rationale for faculty status is embodied in three key principles: (1) academic freedom and tenure, (2) collegial governance, (3) evaluation criteria that match faculty ranks. The University of Illinois at Urbana-Champaign has been among the institutions most committed to faculty status for librarians and most successful in its implementation. 11 notes. J W

75. Smith, Eldred. "Academic Status for College and University Librarians: Problems and Prospects." *College and Research Libraries* 31 (January 1970): 7-13.
Predicts that trends in higher education, the information explosion, etc. will urge recognition of librarians' key role in teaching and research. Changes in the organization of libraries, recruiting of librarians, library

education, and librarian professional activities must be pursued actively for librarians' best contribution to academe to be realized. 28 notes. H

76. Sparks, David G. E. "Academic Librarianship: Professional Strivings and Political Realities." *College and Research Libraries* 41 (September 1980): 408-421.
Summarizes the history of the ACRL Standards and the arguments that have been propounded pro and con, especially regarding tenure and collegiality. Faculty status still requires evaluation in terms of (1) professionalization, (2) power relationships in higher education, and (3) academic collective bargaining. 72 notes. J W

77. "The Three Faces of Eve: Or, the Identity of Academic Librarianship, A Symposium." *Journal of Academic Librarianship* 2 (January 1977): 276-285.
Ten short articles and letters advocating or opposing faculty status. Writers include H. William Axford, R. Dean Galloway, Virgil F. Massman, Robert M. Pierson, and others. Most of these pieces respond to Axford's lead article, which expresses reservations regarding faculty status for librarians. J W

78. Wells, Mary Baier. "Requirements and Benefits for Academic Librarians: 1959-1979" *College and Research Libraries* 43 (November 1982) 450-458.
A study of advertisements for librarian positions in three librarianship journals for the period 1959-1979. This study tested whether expectations of librarians' qualifications rose, the nature of librarian work changed, and whether

salaries increased. In these two decades, educational expectations, in particular, increased, as did responsibilities; salaries, in general followed fiscal trends in academe. J W

79. Wilson, Pauline. "Librarians As Teacher: The Study of an Organization Fiction." *Library Quarterly* 49 (April 1979): 146-162.

The assertion that librarians are teachers is an "organization fiction," i.e., an inaccurate view unquestioningly accepted by a group to serve a particular purpose, such as, improving the group's self-image. This fiction about librarians impedes development of correct professional image and causes contention among librarians. 58 notes. W